Megan —
For YOB Camp
Endeavors

Bless your N.

Joai & Patriu

CU00660181

*Why Blueprints?*

*Christian camping is mushrooming around the globe. The unique expressions that are emerging in Africa, Asia, and Latin America arise from committed, energetic, sacrificial leaders who work tirelessly to share God's love and God's Word with their campers.*

*Christian Camping International (CCI) provides the connection point for information to flow and relationship to blossom within the worldwide Christian camping community. Together, Christian camping leaders from all corners of the world share best practices, face common challenges, and encourage one another.*

*The prayer of Refueling in Flight is that by partnering with CCI and other like-minded ministries, this book will produce a double blessing – a blessing to the readers and a blessing to the leaders of the Christian camping movement worldwide.*

*Visit www.danbolin.com for ordering information - including bulk discounts.*

**Proceeds from BLUEPRINTS will support the Christian camping movement around the world.**

## What people are saying about Blueprints . . .

*Bolin provides the long-term camp leader with poignant perspectives of camp's efficacy, while enlightening the "newbies" of its solid Biblical foundations.*
Dr. Lisa Anderson-Umana (Christian Camping Latin America - USA/ Honduras)

*In the Leadership incubator we know as Camp, biblical principles are lived out daily and many lives are transformed by following these Bible based guidelines. Oh, to have had these clearly laid out before I started my Christian Camping leadership journey.*
Ross Bay (Christian Camping New Zealand)

*Wow, I've found a treasure! While reading Blueprints, I felt totally inspired by the truth of God's Word coming through. So practical, so clear, such a joy to read, such resonance in my spirit.*
Nel Blanken (New Generation - Retired, Jamaica)

*Blueprints is scriptural, practical and motivational; reading it made me want to return to the very camp I attended when the Lord saved me at age 13.*
Peter Reid (Torchbearers International - USA/Germany)

*Never have I encountered anything like Blueprints. It stands alone as a comprehensive and compelling Biblically based defense of this powerful movement of God.*
Bob Kobielush (Christian Camp & Conference Association - Retired, USA)

*When I was reading this book, it was like an inspiration for us. We Christian Camping Nepal are in developing stage though the camping was in our blood. When I was reading this book, I was reminded that we are too writing the camping ministry history for the generations to come.*
John Chhetri (Christian camping leader - Nepal)

*To every Christian camping leader, and all who aspire to that role, here's your book. I'm glad it isn't exclusive to Western culture. Dr. Bolin's well-crafted principles will serve any Believer involved in the fruitful ministry of Christian camping.*
> Dan DeGroat (Global Outreach Group - USA)

*If we think that we invented Christian Camping, think again! This book clearly shows how camping and all its benefits, challenges, learning opportunities and attributes are imbedded in God's creation and his Word.*
> Norman Doney (Christian Camping International-Worldwide, UK)

*This book is a must-own, leaping off your shelf, as a template to overlay any camp history or vision. It measures why and how we desire a particular camp experience, regardless of age or culture. Indeed, it is a quintessential reference for all time.*
> Jim Fletemeier (Fletemeier & Lee Associates - Retired, USA)

*Blueprints is an excellent read for camp leaders of any age. Dan weaves the story of God's Plan and Christian Camping together through Creation, Salvation, Transformation laying a Biblical World View as a foundation to the Why, What and How behind the Power Of Camp.*
> Steve Prudhomme (Grace Adventures - USA)

*Through a balance of Biblical truth drawn from the Word of God linked with his immense practical experience and excellent application to Christian camping, this book will become essential reading for leaders and camp staff everywhere in the years to come.*
> Lorimer Gray (Abernethy Trust - Retired, Scotland)

*Biblically literate and solidly grounded in experience and reflection, it calls us to enter into the joyful and intentional practice of Christian camping as a doorway both to discipleship and mission.*
> Keith Hagon (Christian Residential Network - UK)

*This is a book to pick up, read all the way through, and then read again and again one to always have close at hand!*
> Dan Smith (The Urban Ministry Institute/World Impact - USA)

*Decades of immersion in camping have allowed Dan Bolin to author a comprehensive, insightful, engrossing book which goes to the heart of the question: why camp? He establishes a Biblical framework and unpacks the applications.*
Gary Hill (CRU - Australia)

*A brilliant resource for the global Christian camp community offered by a lifelong camp practitioner and global leader. To Dr. Dan Bolin's pen, God is the ultimate camp leader/director/counselor, forming us, his campers of all dispositions, gender, ages and cultures.*
Dr. Muhia Karianjahi (Wheaton College - Kenya/USA)

*In his book, Blueprints, Dan Bolin clearly explains the biblical foundation behind Christian camping and why it is so effective. Each chapter uses key Scripture passages to explore biblical models of why Christian camping works. May God use this book to train and inspire current and future Christian camping leaders.*
Bruce Dunning (Medeba - Canada)

*Combining his years in Christian Camping with his experience serving camps internationally, Dan lays a biblical foundation for camps around the globe. If you are currently serving at a Christian Camp or considering that path, Dan's expertise makes this book a must read.*
Bob Nunziato (Hartland Camp - USA)

*Dan Bolin is a deep well of scriptural and Christian camping knowledge that we all should be dipping our buckets into for encouragement and professional development. Thank you again, Dan, for this outstanding work.*
Keith Oglesby (Liberty University - USA)

*Dan does an outstanding, simple, and profound job of capturing the holistic genius of what makes camp so effective. His casual, easy reading, and insightful style will excite the brand new summer staffer, re-energize board members, re-affirm veteran staff members, and nurture current and prospective donors.*
Stan White (Christian camping veteran - USA)

Dan Bolin's book, Blueprints, captures the essence of what transpires when someone unplugs from technology and daily life and is placed in an environment where they can encounter Christ.
   Linda Paulk (Sky Ranch - USA)

This book provides over five decades of pure Dan Bolin wisdom, fully integrated with scripture. If you are involved in or passionate about camp ministry as an experienced professional or emerging leader, spend some time over coffee with Dan. It will be worth your while!
   Dr. Rob Ribbe (Wheaton College - USA)

Everyone involved in Christian camping from donor to board member to leader should read this book . . . You will gain a firm Biblical perspective and appreciation for Christian camping.
   Ray Schnickels (Strategic Executive Tools - USA)

This contribution is a wonderful collaboration between Biblical truth, academic discussion, raw practice, and experience of the amazing fruits of temporary community manifested as Christian Camping.
   Dr. Pieter L Snyman (Camp Extreme Life - South Africa)

Using seamless integration of God's Word and good principles of effective Christian camping ministry, Blueprints is long overdue, and I believe will be used by generations of Christian camping leaders to come.
   Aaron Ziebarth (Joy-El - USA)

Dan Bolin has drafted an excellent overview of the power of Christian camping. Like a skilled architect he has erected a well-crafted structure of principals that illuminate why camping is essential for the life of the Church. His "Blueprints" is a much needed contribution in training the next generation of camp counselors and conference center leaders.
   Bedford Holmes (Texas)

Two chapters into Blueprints I found myself thinking, "We need to buy a copy of this book for all of our new staff members at Hume. It's foundational in that it answers the question from scripture, "Why Christian camping?"
   Dathan Brown (Hume Lake Christian Camps)

# BLUEPRINTS

DR. DAN BOLIN

© 2022 Dan Bolin | Refueling in Flight Ministries, Inc

All rights reserved. No part of this book may be reproduced or used in any manner without the prior written permission of the copyright owner, except for the use of brief quotations in a book review. To request permissions, contact the publisher at info@refuelinginflight.com.

**Hardcover:** 979-8-9850725-1-8
**Paperback**: 979-8-9850725-0-1
**E-book:** 979-8-9850725-2-5
**Library of Congress Control Number:** 2021923468

**RIF Publishing**
PO Box 3115
Arlington, VA 22203
www.refuelinginflight.com
First Edition | Arlington VA | 2022

**Scripture References**
Taken from The Holy Bible, New International Version® NIV®
Copyright © 1973 1978 1984 2011 by Biblica, Inc. TM
Used by permission. All rights reserved worldwide.

**Names:** Bolin, Dan, author. | Hendricks, Bill, foreword by.
**Title:** Blueprints
**Subtitle:** Biblical Designs for Christian Camping - Yesterday, Today & Tomorrow

*To Bedford Holmes*

*A great Christian camping leader and a better friend.*

**R**etreats, camps, conferences, and adventure experiences are the places where the people of God, the love of God, the truth of God, and the grace of God intersect. And at that convergence – within the beauty of God's majestic creation – lives are changed forever and ever.

# Contents

# Foreword

*by Bill Hendricks*

My father, Howard G. Hendricks, began teaching at Dallas Theological Seminary in 1951. Right from the start, he was considered a maverick—a reputation he rather enjoyed, to be perfectly honest. He had been asked to start a department for a new discipline (at the time) called "Christian Education." CE was about instructing everyday Christians and their children (the "laity," as they were called) in Bible-related topics and themes. In other words, it meant training future church leaders in how to establish Sunday School programs, youth ministries, and the like.

Believe it or not, that sort of thing was highly suspect among the old guard theologians of that era. For many, Christian Education seemed like a surefire way to open the door to heresy. Why, allow a "layman" (that is, a non-seminarian, a theologically untrained person) to teach the Bible, and before you know it, you'll have no end of false doctrine spreading through your congregation!

On top of that, "Christian Ed" (as people referred to it) seemed too lightweight to hold its own against such deeper-sounding theological disciplines as Christology, soteriology, hamartiology, and eschatology. Christian Ed trafficked in frivolous, if not silly, matters like Bible drills and flannelgraph stories. It just seemed too *fun* to be part of a theological curriculum (where "fun" and "God" were never used in the same sentence).

But Dad was not the least bit deterred by any of that noise. He just went in and taught every day, and by the time he retired sixty years later, an estimated 10,000 seminarians had sat in his classes.

One of the earliest of those classes was Christian Camping. It may not have been the only seminary course in the country on that subject, but if there were others, there certainly weren't many. I was a young boy when Dad created that course, and even I thought it sounded like way too much fun for a graduate-level class. Dad invited me to come along with his students whenever they would do the on-site portion of the course at a nearby camp (where I used to go in the summers). To my eyes, Christian camping meant going out in the boondocks to explore and hike around, tie knots, chop wood, build campfires, cook great food, sing songs, tell jokes, enjoy the sunset, and hear about

Jesus. What was not to like? I mean, if you were a student, how could you possibly ever fail such a course?

Years later, I learned that behind all the fun in Christian camping is a very serious and very momentous purpose. And when I discovered that purpose, I realized that there's actually a biblical term for camping: it's what we call *the wilderness.*

Now most people think of the wilderness as a place of hardship and pain. They think of a parched, stony desert, a barren wasteland only fit for the extremes of humanity—the very worst (thieves, bandits, outlaws), the worst off (the outcasts, the extremely poor, the lepers, the demon-possessed), or the holiest (ascetics, anchorites, hermits). There's no fun in the wilderness.

True, but remember I said that Christian camping is actually about something *behind* the fun. In a similar way, the wilderness is actually about something *behind* the hardship and pain. Yes, a wilderness experience may be arduous (although it doesn't have to be), but its genius lies in taking people out of their standard routines and rhythms, unplugging them from all the distracting voices and influences and systems and connectedness, disrupting their "normal" life in order to create margin—a place and a space where they can encounter God.

Looked at from that point of view, camping has been around a long time. At least all the way back to when God told Abram, "Leave Haran." In obedience, Abram left Haran. And where did he go? He went camping ("wildernessing," if you will) in a land called Canaan. There in Canaan, Abraham (as he was by then called) believed God, and it was credited to him as righteousness.

Abraham's grandson, Jacob, had a similar experience. He got crosswise with his half-brother, Esau, so he headed off to "camp" (a wilderness experience). There he found someone to marry (as occasionally happens at camp), but more importantly he wrestled with God. That wrestling match changed Jacob's life.

Jacob's sons eventually relocated from Canaan to Egypt, and several hundred years later, one of their descendants, Moses, grew up in the palace of the Pharaoh. One day he found himself in serious trouble, so he ran away, ending up at Camp Horeb, also known as the mountain of God. And what does the text say? "There the angel of the LORD appeared to him." Again, an encounter with God proved to be life-changing for the camper.

Perhaps the ultimate camper was David. As a shepherd-boy, we could almost say that David grew up at camp. If you spend any time reading the Psalms attributed to David, you realize this man must have had countless encounters with God in the wilds of nature while growing up. "If I ascend to heaven (if I go up), You are there. If I descend to Sheol (if I go down), You are there. If I were to fly away on the wings of the dawn (go east), I would find You there. If I settled down on the other side of the sea (go west), I would even find You there." Who writes something like that except someone who has spent plenty of time at camp—time away from "normal" society in the outdoors?

David's son ruled over the zenith of Israel's dynasty, but his grandson was a fool and lost ten of the Twelve Tribes to a rival kingdom. Under a succession of increasingly bad kings, both peoples turned further and further away from God. So He sent prophets to warn them. The greatest of those prophets was Elijah, who, in a single day, called down fire from heaven, oversaw the execution of 450 prophets of Baal, ended a three-year drought, and outran Ahab's chariot for 25 miles from Mount Carmel back to Jezreel.

By the end of that day, the queen had put out a contract on Elijah, and he fled for his life. He traveled more than 100 miles to the south and then another day's journey beyond that until he fell down, completely spent and utterly hopeless. By God's intervention Elijah rested and then ate, and then he traveled forty more days until he, like Moses before him, ended up at Camp Horeb, the mountain of God. Like Moses, Elijah encountered the soft whisper of God in that place.

Biblical stories of camping are endless. Think of Jonah, the prophet who went to a coastal camp for his encounter with God. Consider John the Baptist, who, like David, essentially grew up at camp. How else do you explain his preference for locusts and wild honey? Jesus Himself was led by the Holy Spirit to experience forty days (and nights) of "wildernessing" (camping)—only instead of encountering God, He had to engage Satan! Likewise, after Saul's (Paul's) dramatic conversion on the Damascus Road, he headed east for a season at Camp Arabia, where God revealed His plan to unite Jew and Gentile as one in Christ.

In short, Christian camps change lives for the same reason the wilderness changes lives: people encounter God there. There's a gracious mystery in play by which God uses the disruptive nature of camp to sneak up on a camper's blind side and tell them things and show them things and implant things deeply in their soul that He most wants them to know and experience.

Those stodgy theologians who disparaged Christian camping as frivolous were missing the point. Christian camping is not about the fun, it's about life-change. It's about people meeting God—often for the very first time. If all the activities and games and contests and skits and jokes and cheers and songs and food and counselors and the rest of the camping experience serve that purpose—then yes, camping may be fun, but it's *serious fun*!

And for that reason, Christian camping should be taken seriously. It's too important to be done carelessly or without a proper understanding.

No one is better suited to provide us with that understanding than my lifelong friend, Dan Bolin. I met Dan in May 1971 when he came to Texas to work at Pine Cove for its fourth summer of operation. Dan was as tall as a redwood tree, with hair as red as a sunset, freckles like red pepper flakes all over his face and neck, and a smile as captivating as a tractor beam. At the end of training week, when it was time to assign him a camp name, someone volunteered the thought that he was known to enjoy hiking in the mountains. That led to a brainstorming session about all the things hikers do in the mountains. Suddenly someone blurted out, "Yodel!" And with that, Dan Bolin became Yodel to me and generations of other staff and campers at Pine Cove and beyond.

I worked at Pine Cove over its first six summers, but Dan stayed on for 25 years. He opened the Towers Camp for elementary age kids, then he became Program Director, and after that Executive Director and a Board member. After Pine Cove, Dan began consulting with camping leaders nationwide, and then he moved into an international sphere of influence through Christian Camping International.

I review this history to point out that Dan speaks out of a lifetime of experience with camps of every kind, in every possible setting in the world. It's arguable that no one else alive today brings as much breadth and depth to the subject of Christian camping than Dan Bolin. Moreover, because Dan has to be among the most teachable people I know, he contains the wisdom he's gathered from countless conversations with guides and mentors who have poured into him what they know, what they don't know, what they can only guess at, what they hope for, and what they most pray about. To my mind, that's priceless, and it makes *Blueprints* an invaluable contribution to the church's understanding and practice of camping.

I have to warn you, though: when it comes to communicating truth, Dan has an uncanny way of under-promising and over-delivering. What I mean is that he's a master of the technique my dad always urged his students to employ: put the cookies on the lower shelf. In other words, package what you have to say in such a way that even a 5th-grader can understand it. Then let the truth work its magic. I've seen Dan do that time and again in his talks, his writings, and his stories. He says something very simple—so simple you think it's too simple. And then—*wham!* You suddenly realize the significance of what he's talking about, and it changes your whole outlook. Trust me, you'll find that penchant for wrapping brilliant insight in simple terms constantly at work in *Blueprints*.

I could not be prouder of Dan for writing this book! First of all, because it brings together and articulates what he knows by firsthand experience. It's not a book, it's a life-message. We're getting to read something right out of his soul.

Secondly, Dan is passing on to younger leaders and future generations what he knows and has learned—often from some very tough, very expensive tuition. That's exactly what we need more of in the world, and most especially in the church. If what he shares here helps one leader avoid one major pitfall and/or make one major gain they otherwise would not have made, that would be worth it all.

Thirdly—and selfishly—I love what Dan is doing here because he's building on the legacy of my dad. Dan was one of those 10,000 students at Dallas Seminary who sat under Dad's teaching, and in fact Dan eventually became a faculty member himself and taught the Christian camping course for more than twenty years. So I can assure you that Dad would be ecstatic over this book. Indeed, were he still alive and teaching that course, he would immediately install *Blueprints* as the required text.

Fourthly, and finally, I am delighted with this book because I have the privilege of knowing Dan as a valued friend. We met at Pine Cove and share countless memories from those years (not the least of which is playing guitars and singing with our partner in crime, Tilly). But we've also shared losses and tears together over family members who've passed away. We've seen friends get married and divorced. We've celebrated victories and commiserated in defeats. We've compared notes about publishing books (I mostly babble about the craft of writing books, Dan shares wisdom about actually selling books). We've fumed, pontificated, and laughed about the state of the church in America and cheered with excitement over the explosion of the church globally. We've envisioned schemes that could change the world (if we were kings), as well as lent each other timely perspective when needed about simply and humbly stewarding our five loaves and two fishes.

In short, by asking me to write this foreword, Dan has shown me what he has always shown me since the day I first met him in 1971—the loyalty, trust, and generosity of a true friend. What could be worth more than that? So I am deeply honored to be included in this project. And I am further honored to now invite you to enter into the unique and patiently gained wisdom of my special friend, Dan Bolin

Bill Hendricks
President, The Global Centre for Giftedness
Dallas, Texas

# Preface

As a four-year-old, I was a little too young to attend the three-day day camp at Mt. Tabor Park in Portland, Oregon. But the ministry leaders needed volunteers and the only way my mother could help was if I came along; so, they agreed. Life has never been the same.

I was blessed to spend most of my childhood going to camp, counting down the days until camp, or reflecting on great memories from camp. Summers during my youth were spent volunteering at Christian residential camps or more often, helping wilderness backpacking ministries. My adult life has been invested deeply in Christian camping, 25 summers at Pine Cove, from cabin counselor to executive director. During those years I benefited greatly from 12 years on the board of Christian Camping International – USA, two of those years as board chair. For about 10 years I consulted with numerous Christian camps in the United States and Canada. My final career stop was as the International Director of Christian Camping International. I was privileged to serve in that role for 11 years. I've also had the privilege of serving as an adjunct professor at Dallas Theological Seminary for over 20 years teaching students the methods and values of Christian camping.

I've been blessed. And we are blessed to be a blessing.

## *Blueprints*

Every building project starts with a plan. Possibly a sketch on the back of an old envelope or a pencil drawing on a notepad. The greater the magnitude and significance of the project, the more planning and forethought is required. A blueprint describes the plan in detail and illustrates the interconnectedness between support structures, electrical grid, plumbing connections, lighting, floor plan, and aesthetics for the entire project.

The word blueprint has become a common metaphor for thoughtful design. Not surprisingly, God, as the Master Designer, has provided some blueprints for Christian camping leaders to use as they plan and build their ministries. This book explores several biblical passages – blueprints – that will help Christian camping leaders understand and implement highly effective camping programs.

## Hopes for the Book

The hope for **Blueprints** is three-fold. *First* and foremost, I want to share some reflections from God's word that I consider foundational to the ministry of Christian camping. These passages provide timeless principles that each culture and each generation must apply to its unique context. The key is to always ground our methodology on the bedrock truth of scripture. Many excellent resources are available to help Christian camping leaders learn best practices and employ effective techniques to run high quality camp ministries. The Christian camping movement will always benefit from proven, professional training. However, the foundation upon which the ministries are built is critical. Without a solid base, the superstructure will never be properly aligned. My hope is that the truth of God's word will always be the basis upon which the movement builds its programs and operations.

*Second*, I'm an American and I write from that perspective. However, I have dear friends who serve in exceptional camp ministries around the globe. As I toured the world, visiting Christian camps, I discovered that the highly effective camp ministries were the ones that found culturally relevant expressions for the movement that engaged the unique realities of their contexts. In this book, I try to provide universal principles that can be applied in any culture. I may write with an American filter, but my hope is that the biblical truth about Christian camping will find creative and effective expressions in every corner of the world.

*Third*, I've heard a lot of 'Chicken Little' fans crying *the sky is falling*. Some voices persist in declaring that the days of Christian camping are in the rearview mirror, and it is a ministry style that has run its course. When we focus on techniques, there is a level of truth to those frightening projections, methodologies come and go; they all have a *use-by* date. But when we look deeply at God's design for life and ministry, the Christian camping world has little to fear. We enthusiastically forge ahead. The best is yet to come.

## Limitations

It may be helpful to say a few words about what this book is *not*. *First*, no resource can deal with all the issues facing Christian camping. There are many topics related to this great industry that others will need to address. I pray that leaders in the next generation will step forward with biblically refined answers to the ever-emerging challenges within the ever changing landscape.

*Second*, it is not the voice of God. The title, **Blueprints**, is very intentionally plural. There is not one blueprint that completely captures God's intent. Each passage offers its own layer of biblical perspective. Collectively, these twelve chapters explore the principles that comprise a strong biblical basis for the Christian camping movement. However, I do not want to state, suggest, or imply that I speak for God. These perspectives are humbly submitted as my best thoughts on the selected passages. I am always eager for improvement.

*Third*, this book is not intended to be the end-all in any discussion about the nature of Christian camping and God's design for this unique ministry. I hope that this book will foster extended biblically based conversations about the intentionality and effectiveness of Christian camping.

---

*Dear God,*

*Please blow away any chaff of my inaccuracies or human biases contained within this book. Please allow the kernels of biblical truth on these pages to fall upon the fertile soil of Christian camping leaders around the world. And Father, please allow Christian camping to continue the joy of seeing you change lives and produce a great harvest for your glory. Amen!*

---

*Three times a year all your men must appear before the Lord your God at the place he will choose: at the Festival of Unleavened Bread, the Festival of Weeks and the Festival of Tabernacles.*

*Deuteronomy 16:16*

## Chapter One
# The Pillars of Camp
*Deuteronomy 16:16*

One way to look at the story of the Bible is through the lens of Christian camping.

- A young man went to camp.
- He spent a great deal of time with the animals.
- He met a pretty girl.
- They spent time together tending the camp garden.
- In the evenings they went on hikes and enjoyed deep conversations with the Camp Director.
- Then they broke the camp's only rule and got kicked out!
- The rest of the Bible explains how the Camp Director paid an excruciating price to offer full scholarships to anyone who would like to return to camp.

Growing up, I loved to go to camp, and I lived to go to camp. All year I longed for the freedom from home, the break from routines, and the escape from responsibilities. Even as a young child, camp captured my heart. And it lasted a whole week!

And it lasted my whole life!

My escape was not total. My father volunteered on the camp staff, so I was not far from his watchful eye. But I enjoyed a wonderful week of relative independence unlike any of the other 51 weeks of the year.

We were out-of-doors, swimming in the river, hiking among the Douglas fir, running through freshly mowed fields, and sitting around a campfire. The immersion in God's creation soothed every fiber of my being.

I still remember the names of some of the boys in my cabin. We haven't talked in well over 50 years, but I'm sure we would recall many fond memories and reconnect around our shared experiences.

The spiritual decisions at camp were significant, at least for me. I memorized enough verses to win a small New Testament (that I still have). And I hung on every word during Mr. Birch's story time. I can still recall lessons from Mr. Foss' Bible studies – the Fruit of the Spirit, Elijah, and Daniel. Mr. Peach told missionary stories of places I never expected to visit. And the singing around campfires echoes even today.

So, why camp? How and when did this get started? What is the essence that makes this outdoor ministry so effective? Why is outdoor ministry a high calling?

## Background of Christian Camping

Let's start with a little historical and biblical perspective. Christian camping is not an American invention of the 19th and 20th centuries. It does not find its roots in the early North American contributions of Phillip Gunn, Joseph Rothrock, or George Hinckley. Its genesis is not found in the camp meetings of the Second Great Awakening, the monastic life of the Middle Ages, or the aestheticism of the Desert Fathers. It can be argued that each of these factors contributed to the current expressions of Christian camping, but none explains the movement as well as God's Word. The Bible helps us see how God designed us to be campers and explains the context into which He placed us. Simply put, Christian camping finds it roots in scripture, and it is effective when we conduct camp programs in a way that reflects God's purposeful design.

Viewing scripture through the lens of Christian camping can be like listening to a one-string banjo. Reinterpreting every passage from the vantage point of Christian camping is unfair and inaccurate. The Bible is not about Christian camping, it is about the glory of God revealed in His Son, Jesus Christ, who came and died to save us from the effects of our sin.

Scripture reveals more than the *what* of God's plan and activity; it demonstrates the *how* as well. The pages of the Bible divulge God's heart, His designs, and the tools He employs to accomplish His purposes. This book examines several passages of scripture to discern the methods that God has established to work in our hearts, draw us to Himself, and help us grow into the people He wants us to become. My hope is that this examination will reveal how

Christian camping aligns with God's design for ministry and helps provide biblical support for the movement in the days ahead.

## *The Tapestry of Christian Camping*

So, when did this Christian camping thing begin? The starting point is actually irrelevant if we recognize that the elements associated with the movement today were woven into the tapestry of humanity from the very beginning. Understanding that camping has been with us from the start explains why the children of Israel, Jesus and His disciples, the Desert Fathers, Irish monks, organizers of Revivalist camp meetings, and today's Christian camping leaders are cut from the same fabric. God graciously and skillfully wove camp-like events into the tapestry of human experience. We were designed to be campers. We cannot escape the reality of our make-up, but we can express it either poorly or magnificently.

*God commanded the children of Israel to take breaks from the routines and pressures of their lives and travel to Jerusalem for extended opportunities for worship and relationship building.*

Let's look at one example that demonstrates this basic design that God used for His purposes in the life of the Israelite community.

Relationships develop quickly and deeply at camp. So, to establish community for the children of Israel, God designed camp-like experiences for them throughout the year. It was within a camp context that God planned for the Israelites to grow and develop as a nation. The children of Israel were commanded to attend Camp Jerusalem three times a year. Their camp didn't resemble today's modern facilities with ropes courses, horseback riding, and swimming pools, but their ancient experience included the essential elements that we still employ today.

Three times in the books of Moses, Exodus 23:17, Exodus 34:22-24, and Deuteronomy 16:16, God commanded the children of Israel to take breaks from the routines and pressures of their lives and travel to Jerusalem for extended opportunities for worship and relationship building. Deep spiritual and cultural significance welled up within the Jewish community during these festivals, but transformation also took place in the lives of individuals and families through meaningful and memorable moments. These events, like the camp experiences of today, share five basic elements that I call the Five Pillars of Camp:

- Change of location
- Extended time outside of life's routine
- Immersion into creation

- Relational bonding
- Spiritual intents

### First, place matters.

Home, with its routines and comfortable surroundings, allows us to live life on autopilot. In familiar surroundings and within comfortable routines, we find the safety to hide from moments of introspection, inspiration, and challenge. Mediocrity and normalcy rule in the familiar patterns of everyday life. However, new surroundings engage our senses, setting our awareness radar on high alert. Within new and unfamiliar environments, we become sensitive to the details around us. And that fresh awareness allows us to evaluate old patterns, healthy and unhealthy, that we accept as the norm. Three times a year the children of Israel looked at life from a new and strategic vantage point, allowing them to assess the common place of their lives from God's holy and wise perspective.

### Second, people need time to unwind.

We forget that people who lived thousands of years ago dealt with the same tension and pressure of deadlines, priorities, schedule conflicts, and threats to their livelihood that we face today. Camp for the Israelites provided time off from their obligations and responsibilities just like it does for us. They took several days off at three junctures in their annual calendar. For them a week sufficed. For some of us a long weekend may be adequate, while others may need a two-week vacation. We should all build reflective moments into the routine of our daily lives, but we also need periodic extended times where we enjoy a reprieve from the mundane and the pressures of life.

---

*On the side of a stream, at the base of a mountain, in a forest glade, God speaks through what He has made. And Christian camps provide the context for that to happen.*

---

### Third, God speaks through His creation.

The children of Israel lived in a different world than we experience today. Each time they traveled they were called to walk the roads to Jerusalem, enjoying the idyllic fields, vineyards, and pastures they passed during their pilgrimage. They climbed hills, viewed mountains, forded streams, and slept under a heaven filled with brilliant stars. All the way they marveled at the glory of God displayed in His creation.

Today as more and more people migrate to larger and more densely populated cities, Satan enjoys the easy task of muting creation's proclamation of God's glory. Everywhere we look, asphalt, glass, concrete, and steel proclaim the glory of humanity. All day, smog, haze, and high-rise buildings block the blue sky and shimmering sun. All night, electric lights reflect off the stratosphere dimming the majesty of the moon and stars.

People need time away. But those times away must involve immersion into God's creation, not another hotel setting with recycled air in the heart of a big city. They need places that provide easy access to God's general revelation that is persistently proclaimed through the beauty of His creation. On the side of a stream, at the base of a mountain, in a forest glade, God speaks through what He has made. And Christian camps provide the context for that to happen.

### Fourth, people are designed for relationships.

Times away in the beauty of God's creation provide a powerful catalyst for establishing and deepening healthy relationships. At Camp Jerusalem the children of Israel enjoyed time with their nuclear family and embraced their extended families as well. They reengaged with distant members of their tribes and bonded as a nation.

Relationships thrive at Christian camps between campers, among staff, and with campers and staff. Often, life-long friendships emerge. I met my wife while we worked together on summer staff at a Christian camp, and we have been married over 45 years!

Family camps, couples' conferences, and a host of other camp events create bonding experiences for families and church members. Temporary communities are often much more than momentary interactions. Camping's mountain-top moments create brief times of unity, but those experiences are the foundations that deepen and strengthen the long-lasting relationships within families, churches, and communities.

---

*The Bible presents eternal, unchanging truth, that must be applied to the ever changing and fluid cultural realities we face.*

---

### Fifth, spiritual intents must guide the process.

The children of Israel did not migrate to Jerusalem together three times a year just for a vacation in a new setting – they came to meet with God. Void of spiritual intents, camp is merely an enjoyable holiday and a healthy break from the demands of life. Not bad, but not good enough.

Camp is about sharing the Gospel, living our faith, making commitments, learning deeper truths, and overcoming sin. Every camp has its own focus. Some reach out to the unsaved, focusing on evangelism; others emphasize discipling believers or team building with those who share our faith. Still others have a narrow purpose to help people overcome a specific sin, face a particular challenge, or engage a unique opportunity. And some strive to develop the next generation of Christian leaders. Whatever the strategy, every Christian camp's purpose must align with God's over arching purpose, the fulfillment of the Great Commission.

## Blueprints for Christian Camping

God's word provides numerous patterns for us as we seek to build effective camping ministries. The Bible presents eternal, unchanging truth, that must be applied to the ever changing and fluid cultural realities we face. These biblical principles will be expressed differently in Nepal than in Kenya and look different in Brazil than in New Zealand. But the more our camp programs conform to God's purposeful blueprints, the more effective they will be.

Join me as we explore the *blueprints* for Christian camping that we find in several passages of scripture. As we study these biblical blueprints, we will look at them through the lens of Christian camping, always striving to avoid reading into the text. Rather we will attempt to examine the biblical models to see how God's grand designs can be employed to engage, inspire, and equip each of us to build effective, culturally relevant Christian camping programs.

*The heavens declare the glory of God; the skies proclaim the work of his hands. Day after day they pour forth speech; night after night they reveal knowledge. They have no speech; they use no words; no sound is heard from them. Yet their voice goes out into all the earth, their words to the ends of the world. In the heavens God has pitched a tent for the sun. It is like a bridegroom coming out of his chamber, like a champion rejoicing to run his course. It rises at one end of the heavens and makes its circuit to the other; nothing is deprived of its warmth.*

*__The law of the Lord is perfect,__ refreshing the soul. The statutes of the Lord are trustworthy, making wise the simple. The precepts of the Lord are right, giving joy to the heart. The commands of the Lord are radiant, giving light to the eyes. The fear of the Lord is pure, enduring forever. The decrees of the Lord are firm, and all of them are righteous. They are more precious than gold, than much pure gold; they are sweeter than honey, than honey from the honeycomb. By them your servant is warned; in keeping them there is great reward.*

*But who can discern their own errors? Forgive my hidden faults. Keep your servant also from willful sins; may they not rule over me. Then I will be blameless, innocent of great transgression. __May these words of my mouth and this meditation of my heart be pleasing in your sight, Lord, my Rock and my Redeemer.__*

*Psalm 19*

## Chapter Two
# God's Revelation
*Psalm 19*

Christian camping finds its biblical bedrock in Psalm 19. This foundational passage provides the strength and stability upon which the movement is built. Various expressions of Christian camping have emerged around the world, but the truth of this psalm is the common support for all ministries within the Christian camping community. Let's unpack this seminal passage from a Christian camping perspective.

## God's Revelation through Creation

The psalm begins with a simple, yet profound statement; ***The heavens declare the glory of God*** (Psalm 19:1). David starts this majestic psalm with the forthright observation that God's creation declares His glory! The stars, moon, clouds, rainbows, sunrise, sunset, and sunshine are all town criers, proclaiming the glory of God throughout the world. God's glory is displayed continually and comprehensively around the globe. The first six verses of this powerful and instructive psalm focus on God's self-revelation through creation. Bottom line, God chose creation to reveal His glory.

*There are no hidden valleys or remote islands that the declaration of God's glory does not reach. No political power or human despot can restrict its proclamation. As far as creation's declaration of God's glory, there are no unreached people.*

A common Hebrew figure of speech uses a small part to represent a larger whole – a city for the nation or a leader for the tribe. The heavens, one portion of God's creation, stand for all that God has made. Creation reveals the Creator. Trees, rivers, mountains, meadows, deserts, oceans, and flowers all join the choir heralding the glory of their Creator!

David continues, **Day after day they pour forth speech; night after night they display knowledge. There is no speech or language where their voice is not heard. Their voice goes out into all the earth, their words to the ends of the world** (Psalm 19:2-4a).

Four things are true of the message. *First,* the message is **continual**. The proclamation is 24/7. **Day after day they pour forth speech; night after night they display knowledge**. All day and all night, creation affirms God's glory. The crimson sunrise gives way to bluebird skies, bright sunshine, and puffy clouds. Occasionally storms roll in and thunder and lightning accent the sky. Sometimes rainbows arch the rain-washed heavens. Then evening arrives with a magnificent sunset melting into a dark starry night, home to an ever expanding or contracting moon. The message never ceases to declare the glory of God.

*Second*, the message *defies the curse of Babel*. Language separates us, inhibiting communication and limiting our ability to share information. But the language barrier is no obstacle for God's creation. *There is no speech or language where their voice is not heard.* The message is equally clear to those whose native tongue is Russian, Chinese, Spanish, Farsi, Cebuano, Hindi, Afrikaans, French or English. The division of language cannot hinder creation's continual proclamation.

*Third*, the message is *ubiquitous*. The message of creation penetrates every corner of the world. There are no hidden valleys or remote islands that the declaration of God's glory does not reach. No political power or human despot can restrict its proclamation. As far as creation's declaration of God's glory, there are no unreached people. *Their voice goes out into all the earth, their words to the ends of the world.*

The clear message of God's glory is continual, night and day (v. 2). Language is no barrier; no translation is needed (v. 3). No place, or people is hidden from this proclamation (v. 4). Every person on the planet has continual access to this amazing announcement.

*Fourth,* the message is obvious. David uses the bridegroom at a wedding and an athletic champion to illustrate his final point that the Creator's announcement should be evident to anyone who opens his or her eyes. *In the heavens he has pitched a tent for the sun, which is like a bridegroom coming forth from his pavilion, like a champion rejoicing to run his course* (vv. 4b-5).

---

 . . . how foolish are those who enjoy the beauty of God's creation and miss the Creator!

---

To understand David's first illustration, we must remember that in the ancient Middle East the focal point of a wedding was not the bride, but the groom. Let's put this illustration into today's context with the bride as the center of attention. Imagine that my wife and I are invited to a wedding, but she has a schedule conflict and cannot attend. So, I represent our family by myself. I return home and that evening we have the following discussion.

Cay:     *How was the wedding?*

Dan:     *Great.*

Cay:     *What was it like?*

Dan:     *Well, there was a wonderful chocolate groom's cake. The flowers were nice. I liked the string quartet. They played Vivaldi.*

Cay:     *Was the bride beautiful?*

| Dan: | (after a thoughtful pause) *I'm not sure they had one of those at this wedding.* |
| Cay: | *WHAT?!?!?!* |

How absurd! How can you go to a wedding and miss the bride?! The central focus of a wedding is the bride. To miss the bride is to miss the heart of the event. So too, how foolish are those who enjoy the beauty of God's creation and miss the Creator!

David next compares the sun to a world class athlete. Imagine that your friend attends the Olympics and has tickets to the track and field finals. You ask him who won the gold medal in the 100-meter race. He replies, *There were a lot of runners. It was very exciting, lots of flags and cheering, but I don't know if they had a champion this year!* Once again, how absurd! To view the race and miss the champion is as ridiculous as standing in awe of creation and missing the Creator.

However, just because the proclamation of God's glory is continual, defies the curse of Babel, and is ubiquitous and obvious does not mean that it is always makes an impact on people's lives. Satan loves to reduce our awareness of God's glory and limit our knowledge of His majesty. He begins by turning down the volume on creation.

The modern world mutes the voice of creation in four ways. *First, urbanization* has distanced people from God's creation. Today, more than 80% of the world's population lives in urban or suburban settings. This is a significant change from 1950 when just 40% of the world's population lived in cities.[1] This monumental population shift has moved people away from the hills, fields, trees, and rivers of God's creation and into the concrete, steel, glass and asphalt of man-made cities. While creation declares the glory of God, cities mute the message while declaring the glory of humanity.

Second, pollution obscures our view of creation. Smog and haze have dimmed our awareness of creation's heavenly message, but the worst offender is light pollution. The bright lights of cities dim the dazzling display of the nighttime stars. Smog and haze in urban areas conceal the blue skies and sunshine even on cloudless days. Tall buildings block the horizon and hide the majestic and creative sunrises and sunsets. The effect is not just our loss of aesthetics and wonder, we also miss the ongoing revelation of God's glory.

In the early morning hours of January 17, 1994, a 6.7 magnitude earthquake rumbled through Los Angeles, killing more than 50 people and doing billions of dollars of damage to buildings, roads, and utilities, leaving the city in total darkness. Some people left their rattled homes to find safety and check for damage; they were stunned by the ink-black darkness. Several called 911 to report a mysterious cloud hovering over the city. Eventually, the mystery was solved when it was determined that the sinister cloud was the Milky Way. People living in urban settings see a few stars and a diminished moon, but the magnificence of creation is lost, and the powerful message is reduced to a mumble.

*Third*, our *hectic schedules* limit our times to escape the concrete, glass, steel, and asphalt to revel in the majesty of what God has made. We honor busy schedules and feel guilty if we linger in an outdoor setting. Balance between responsible work and intentional relaxation is difficult to sustain. Our compact schedules relegate moments of wonder to special occasions. Glimpses of God's majesty are limited to infrequent forays into the countryside, away from the pressures and projects that dominate our lives.

*Fourth*, the common *mechanistic and materialistic assumptions* about the physical world have created a mental default position leading many to think that all this just happened. Somehow, people assume that nothing became something, something became life, and life became humanity. Many have accepted a world view that no longer needs a Creator.

To fight back against this mind-set, I try to discipline myself to never utter the word n-a-t-u-r-e. Instead, I use the word, *creation*. I deliberately strive to remind myself that there is nothing *natural* about this world; what we see is the *supernatural* creation of the Almighty God. This world is not a beginning and end unto itself, rather it is a splendid gift for us to enjoy and steward. The beauty around us is given from the hands of the glorious Creator-God, and all creation declares His glory.

## God's Revelation through Scripture

David pivots from the discussion of God's revelation through creation to God's revelation through His Word. He begins the second segment of his psalm (v:7-11), *The law of the Lord*. The transition is abrupt and significant. David begins to unpack a second method God uses to reveal Himself to us – the Bible.

Remember, as David writes this psalm, he has little more than the first five books of the Old Testament. No Gospels, no epistles, no Proverbs. Basically, the glowing comments he makes about scripture refer to Genesis, Exodus, Leviticus, Numbers, and Deuteronomy. We occasionally interact with the stories of Genesis and Exodus but rarely read Leviticus, study Numbers, or meditate on Deuteronomy. We seldom go to those books for comfort or soul care. But David will describe these books as *more valuable than gold and sweeter than honey*.

David's structure is simple and direct. He uses six names for God's Word, six descriptions of the Bible, and six benefits or qualities of scripture.[2]

> The law of the LORD is perfect, reviving the soul. The statutes of the LORD are trustworthy, making wise the simple. The precepts of the LORD are right, giving joy to the heart. The commands of the LORD are radiant, giving light to the eyes. The fear of the LORD is pure,

*enduring forever. The ordinances of the LORD are sure and altogether righteous. (vv. 7-9)*

The six names, six descriptions, and six benefits or qualities can be seen in the table below.

| NAME | DESCRIPTION | BENEFIT - QUALITY |
|---|---|---|
| The *Law* of the Lord | Is Perfect | Reviving the Soul |
| The *Statutes* of the Lord | Are Trustworthy | Making the Wise SImple |
| The *Precepts* of the Lord | Are Right | Giving Joy to the Heart |
| The *Commands* of the Lord | Are Radiant | Giving Light to the Eyes |
| The *Fear* of the Lord | Is Pure | Enduring Forever |
| The *Ordinances* of the Lord | Are Sure | And Altogether Righteous |

Have you ever been running on empty, out of gas, or tired physically, emotionally, and spiritually? God's Word can revive your soul! Have you ever been confused, overwhelmed, or faced circumstance too complex for you? God's Word makes wise the simple! Have you ever been discouraged, grieving, or embittered? God's Word gives joy to the heart! Have you ever needed direction, felt lost, or bewildered? God's Word gives light to the eyes!

The Word of God has stood – and will stand – the test of time; it *endures forever*. The truth of the Bible applies to all generations. Every word, every sentence, every chapter is **altogether righteous** and has value for our lives.

The first four stanzas deal with scripture's impact on our lives whereas the final two, enduring forever and altogether righteous, focus on the nature of the Bible itself. The point here is that God has spoken to us through His Word and has told us who He is, what He has done for us, how we can know Him, and what He expects from us.

---

*Camp immerses campers and guests into the majesty of creation and provides compressed times for focused biblical instruction and application. The alignment of God's revelation through both His creation and His Word generates a powerful and effective force that God uses to transform lives for His glory.*

---

David goes on to describe the value and benefits of God's Word. **They are more precious than gold, than much pure gold; they are sweeter than honey, than honey from the comb. By them is your servant warned; in keeping them there is great reward** (vv. 10-11).

No one knows for sure, but I believe David writes this during his reign as king. As the national monarch he knows the value of gold – much fine gold. The Bible is more valuable than pure gold (v. 10a). And then his mind drifts back to his days as a shepherd boy. He remembers the exhilaration of raiding a beehive and enjoying the sweet rewards. God's Word is sweeter than honey – the best honey in the comb (v. 10b).

The Word of God is valuable and sweet for two reasons – the pages are filled with *warnings* and *rewards* (v. 11). The Bible provides direction to protect us from the dangers of life, and it describes the benefits of following God's design. David knew this as well as anyone. In his early years, while obeying God as Saul relentlessly pursued him, he enjoyed God's protection. But when he rebelled against God's commands, as in the story of Bathsheba and Uriah, pain and anguish overwhelmed him.

Camp provides both the *lecture hall* and the *laboratory* for God's Word to be taught and applied. Morning devotions, Bible studies, discussion and story times, testimonies, and campfires are all opportunities for campers to learn the Word of God. But games, activities, meals, conversations, and reflection times allow God's Word to be applied to the routines and realities of life.

Camp is a powerfully effective tool not only because of the creative programing, the well-trained staff members, the beautiful buildings, and the delicious food. Those are all important but not the core. The effectiveness of Christian camping is found in the confluence of these two great methods through which God has chosen to reveal Himself. Camp immerses campers and guests into the majesty of creation and provides compressed times for focused biblical instruction and application. The alignment of God's revelation through both His creation and His Word generates a powerful and effective force that God uses to transform lives for His glory.

## Our Response and Transformation

The third and concluding section of this psalm addresses reflection, commitment, and life transformation.

*Who can discern his errors? Forgive my hidden faults. Keep your servant also from willful sins; may they not rule over me. Then will I be blameless, innocent of great transgression. May the words of my mouth and the meditation of my heart be pleasing in your sight, O LORD, my Rock and my Redeemer. (v. 12-14)*

David explores the depth of his soul when he asks, **Who can discern his errors?** Camps and retreats provide time for introspection but more than just time, these two great sources of God's revelation – creation and the Bible – provide the plumb line by which we can evaluate our lives. Billy Graham wrestled with God all night at Forest Home, a leading camp and conference center in southern California, before settling his commitment to believe the Bible, obey it, and preach it faithfully. Reflecting on that moment he said, *I sensed the presence and power of God as*

*I had not sensed it in months. Not all my questions were answered, but … I knew a spiritual battle in my soul had been fought and won.*[3]

The hope of a new, fresh, and more Christ-like life leads campers to a point of commitment. Camp is often the place where God draws people into a new relationship with Himself. Camp is also the place where many Christians, young and old, recommit to live more Christ-like lives and turn from the addictive power of sin. David says, *Keep your servant also from willful sins; may they not rule over me* (v. 13).

Having reflected on God's revelation through both creation and the Bible and touching on introspection and commitment, David prays for transformation. He says, *May the words of my mouth and the meditations of my heart be pleasing in your sight, O LORD* (v. 14).

Once again, Hebrew poetry is in play. The words of our mouths represent much more than spoken sounds. This imagery includes all our outward expressions. All our behavior and actions should bring honor to God. Similarly, *the meditations of my heart* represent the motives and hidden thoughts that spur our attitudes and actions. David wants to be a different man. He wants to please God in how he expresses his life to the public and in the secret areas known only to himself and God. He wants to live a God-honoring life from the inside out.

David concludes his prayer with two powerful and perceptive names for God. He addresses God as my **Rock** and my **Redeemer.** The word **Rock** brings to mind God's power and strength, and the word **Redeemer** focuses on God's loving relationship with us.

One of the Hebrew names for God is **Elohim**, it means the **Mighty One**. This name emphasizes the power and strength of God. He is the supreme Ruler over every aspect of His domain. God's authority and protection are associated with the use of the name Elohim. David chooses the image of a rock to evoke thoughts of God's strength and power. He also chose to begin this psalm using Elohim, in verse one, as the name for deity, *The heavens declare the glory of Elohim.*

In verse 7, David shifts terms from GOD (Elohim) to LORD (YHWH). *The law of the LORD is perfect, reviving the soul.* The word LORD is translated from the Hebrew word YHWH. This name for deity is often used when addressing God's covenantal relationship with His people. David's selection of the word YHWH emphasizes God's personal and loving relationship with mankind.

The declaration of God's glory through creation is powerful and significant but it is never enough. We can stand in awe of God as we scan the midnight sky, wade a mountain stream, enjoy the fragrance of a rose, or gaze at a snow-capped peak. But we cannot know Him apart from the revelation of God's Word. God is our Elohim, our **Rock**, our **Mighty One** whose glory we see through creation. But our **Rock** must also be our **Redeemer.** We come to know our **Redeemer** as we interact with the truth of God's Word. We need the redeeming message of the Bible if we are to enter into a relationship with God through His Son, Jesus Christ.

---

*Camp is not a magic pill for life transformation – only God can change a life. However, Christian camp ministry can be a highly effective context within which God works. Camp aligns two of the primary methods God has chosen to reveal Himself to the world, His creation, and His Word.*

---

Camp is a place where children, young people, and adults are immersed into the revelation of God through His creation and His Word. We may be awestruck by the revelation of God our **Rock**, but we enter a new and deeper relationship with our **Redeemer** as we encounter the truth of His Word. And as transformation occurs, ***the words of our mouths and the meditations of our hearts become acceptable in the sight of our Rock and Redeemer.***

Camp is not a magic pill for life transformation – only God can change a life. However, Christian camp ministry can be a highly effective context within which God works. Camp aligns two of the primary methods God has chosen to reveal Himself to the world, His creation, and His Word.

Camp experiences intertwine the dual revelations of God as our Rock and Redeemer. And each year God uses these two powerful forces to establish, deepen, and strengthen His relationship with millions of people around the world.

The LORD God formed the man from the dust of the ground and breathed into his nostrils the breath of life, and the man became a living being.

*Genesis 2:7*

The LORD God took the man and put him in the Garden of Eden to work it and take care of it. And the LORD God commanded the man, "You are free to eat from any tree in the garden; but you must not eat from the tree of the knowledge of good and evil, for when you eat of it you will surely die."

*Genesis 2:15-17*

When the woman saw that the fruit of the tree was good for food and pleasing to the eye, and also desirable for gaining wisdom, she took some and ate it. She also gave some to her husband, who was with her, and he ate it. Then the eyes of both of them were opened, and they realized they were naked.

*Genesis 3:6-7a*

So the LORD God banished him from the Garden of Eden to work the ground from which he had been taken. After he drove the man out, he placed on the east side of the Garden of Eden cherubim and a flaming sword flashing back and forth to guard the way to the tree of life.

*Genesis 3:23-24*

## Chapter Three
# God's Design
*Genesis 1-3*

Christian camps find their homes in gorgeous settings and not by accident. Mountains, lakesides, forests, and stream banks provide the beautiful, tranquil, enticing contexts where God works in remarkable ways.

Setting matters!

The rich and famous spend small fortunes buying vacation homes on lovely seaside coves or near the ski slopes of snow-capped mountains. In major cities, apartment rent is higher on *tree-lined* streets. In Russia, families escape the smog and bustle of big cities each weekend to tend their small dachas (farms) in the rural settings outside their towns. In the densely populated megacities of Japan, colorful flowers cascade from the balconies of high-rise apartments.

Why the attraction to beautiful out-of-doors settings? Why spend money to escape the city? Why take the time to travel out of town? And why crowd already limited space with flowers and plants? What is it about beautiful settings and garden amenities that attracts people and engages their spirits? The answer is simple yet profound: *God designed us to live in a Garden.* Our roots run back through the millennia to Genesis 1-3. Many details are shrouded in the mist of antiquity, but one thing is crystal clear, God designed people to live in a Garden.

*The Garden represents our much deeper longings. It embodies our desire to reconnect with God, enjoy healthy relationships with those around us, and find purpose for our lives.*

## Life in the Garden

Four significant realities flow from life in the Garden and explain our desire to return to that marvelous setting. *First*, it was a stunningly beautiful place. *Second*, God and His people enjoyed open, meaningful fellowship. *Third*, people got along with each other. And *fourth*, purpose, joy, and fulfillment energized life.

When sin disrupted and devastated that perfect situation, Adam and Eve's relationship with God was broken, tension flared, and they were forced to leave their idyllic home. With that departure they lost the simple yet profound purpose for their lives. An angel with a flaming sword barred their return. Their marvelous world was lost, but not forgotten. And from that day until now, they – and we, their children – have been searching for the lost Garden. A place of reunion with God, a home where relationships are healthy and supportive, a site of creative beauty, and a life filled with purpose and meaning.

## The Loss of Place

In the United States many people live in single-family houses. Surrounding these homes are green grass and shrubbery. Mowing the lawn, trimming the bushes, watering the grass and flowers, fertilizing at the right time, and raking the leaves consume a great deal of time, money, and attention. So, why do it? Why not just pour concrete and paint it green? And why green? Because we are searching for the Garden. Our desire for awe-inspiring beauty is powerful and universal. Outdoor experiences attract millions of participants each year. They hike, sail, ride, paddle, and climb, engaging the beauty of God's creation. Most are inspired by the magnificent creation, but sadly, many miss the glory of the Creator. The inspiration of the out-of-doors is merely our response to the physical manifestation of God's glory displayed within His handiwork. The Garden represents our much deeper longings. It embodies our desire to reconnect with God, enjoy healthy relationships with those around us, and find purpose for our lives.

## *The Loss of Union with God*

The pristine innocence that mankind enjoyed in the Garden disappeared forever. The union that marked the relationship between God and His people was broken. The spiritual hole in our hearts can never be filled with a faster car, a bigger house, more money, more followers on social media, a prettier wife, more degrees, or stronger liquor. God alone can fill the hollow in our hearts. We all desire to return to that Garden-like personal communion with God.

Despite our sin, God loves us and desires to restore the relationship. To remedy this divide, God, in unimaginable love, sent His one and only Son Jesus to die in our place, pay the penalty of sin, defeat death, and bridge the separation between Himself and His people. Every person on earth is looking for that fulfilling relationship, but most look in the wrong places. False religions call us to work our way to God. False hopes crush our spirits leaving us confused, disappointed, and frustrated. False medications deaden the pain but only for a while. Only Jesus can restore our relationship with God.

---

*Naming animals demonstrated Adam's authority over the lions, lizards, cattle, and caterpillars. And tending the Garden demonstrated mankind's dominion over the floral kingdom.*

---

## The Loss of Community

Adam and Eve where not only the first couple – for who knows how long, they were the entire human race. Their relationship appeared to be loving, caring, and supportive. But with the entrance of sin into the world, their relationship became distorted. Blame, discord, tension, and competition replace the unity and cooperation woven into the original fabric of their relationship. Adam blamed Eve. Eve blamed the snake. Division replaced the unity that once bonded relationships. Within one generation, the interpersonal tension had spiraled downward, and murder entered humanity as a means of resolving conflict.

Without God's restorative work in our souls by His Spirit, our lives revert to self-centered protection. We can easily miss the union of meaningful community and the refreshment of supportive relationships. The result is greater discord, more hostility, increasing violence, and wider separation.

## The Loss of Purpose

While in the Garden, Adam and Eve were given meaningful tasks that filled their days with activity and purpose. Adam named the animals and together, he and Eve tended the Garden. Their supervision of the Garden extended over the animal kingdom and the plant kingdom. Naming animals demonstrated Adam's authority over the lions, lizards, cattle, and caterpillars. And tending the Garden demonstrated mankind's dominion over the floral kingdom. With sin's cataclysmic entry into life's drama, the work and responsibility that previously provided joy and fulfillment soon became a source of sweat and frustration. Carnivorous animals threaten people, tiny mosquitoes annoy humans and spread disease. Thorns and thistles plague the plant kingdoms, and crabgrass infests our lawns. Work in every area became more difficult and less fulfilling.

*Part of humanity's shared DNA is an unconscious desire and unrelenting drive to regain the Garden experience.*

False fulfillments and counterfeit satisfiers rule the day. Comparing our awards, accomplishments, and accumulation to those of others provides a brief and false hope that we are better than most and rank above those we dislike. But at the end of the day, we remain empty. Our attempts to feel better about ourselves prove unsuccessful as we futilely hunt for ways to upgrade our lives.

Since our expulsion from the Garden, mankind has searched for beautiful settings, reconnection with God, significant relationships, and meaningful work. Part of humanity's shared DNA is an unconscious desire and unrelenting drive to regain the Garden experience.

## So, What about Camp?

### Back to the Garden.

Christian camps throughout the world are found along mountain streams, on the shores of placid lakes, in green pastures, and in lush forests. They provide places that attract hearts that are seeking the lost beauty of the Garden. Camp settings provide the opportunity for campers and guests to easily immerse themselves in the majesty of God's creation. The outdoor beauty that surrounds them provides awe and wonder but not as an end within itself. Creation is the North Star, continually point to the Creator. These engagements with creation are woven into the essence of Christian camping. And that is why I prefer the word *creation* to n-a-t-u-r-e.

---

*Unity and diversity flourish as camps focus on the core elements of life and faith. Grace is extended to the weak and received by all. Mistakes are addressed with a view toward improvement and second chances are in generous supply.*

---

### Back to God.

Christian camps offer instruction from God's Word, solitary times of reflection and communion with God, personal and corporate worship experiences, and opportunities to commit – or recommit – to a relationship with Him. Henrietta Mears, the founder of Forest Home and a leading Christian educator said, *Camp is where people make up their minds.* The convergence of God's revelation, through His Word and through His creation, creates a context where hearts are receptive to the message of the Gospel. Camps plan schedules intentionally and coach staff to strategically generate opportunities for loving, life-changing conversations. Those talks provide the openings for deep, eternity-changing decisions. Christian camps generate the setting for campers and guests to reconnect with God, accept His offer of forgiveness, and once again enter into or deepen a personal relationship with Him. And this opportunity to reconnect with God through His Son Jesus is what makes Christian camps Christian.

### Back to Community.

Christian camps are relational. They provide safe places of acceptance, cooperation, teamwork, encouragement, and trust. The brokenness, tension, rivalry, abuse, and distrust that too often mar human relationships are set aside in the Christian camp environment. Unity and diversity flourish as camps focus on the core elements of life and faith. Grace is extended to the weak and received by all. Mistakes are addressed with a view toward improvement and second chances are in generous supply. There, in the beauty of God's creation and within the restoration of a right relationship with God, human relationships grow, flourish, and thrive.

*Camp becomes a greenhouse where godly dreams put down roots and extend branches that will bear fruit for years to come.*

### Back to Purpose.

Christian camps provide meaningful, intentional activities. The camp experience involves instruction, challenge, adventure, independence, experimentation, evaluation, and responsibility. Not free from failure, disappointment, or conflict but within a context of learning, growth and forgiveness. Well-designed camps provide places where activity has purpose, challenges can be overcome, effort rewarded, and evaluated failures become stepping stones for personal and community growth. Campers and staff members have opportunity to explore their gifting and learn new skills. Camp becomes a greenhouse where godly dreams put down roots and extend branches that will bear fruit for years to come. Camp allows campers and staff to learn about themselves, discover God's gifts, and begin the process of building their lives to fulfill their calling.

## Conclusion

Years ago, I stopped to say good-bye to a father, loading his car at the end of a week of family camp. I thanked him for attending and let him know how much I appreciated his family's involvement during the week. His comment was, *Yes, it was a great week. Now back to the real world.* I waved to the car as it rolled toward the big city and thought about that comment a long time. Actually, camp is much more the real world than the world he was reengaging. What makes reality real? Maybe it is how well we align our lives with God's original design and His intent for how we are to live.

So, the history of the world in four simple segments. *First*, God created us to live in a Garden filled with beauty, closeness to Him, healthy relationships with others, and purpose in life. *Second*, Adam and Eve's sinful choice led to our eviction from the Garden, a broken relationship with God, strained human relationships, and the loss of purpose. *Third*, God provided reconciliation through the death and resurrection of His Son Jesus. This climactic moment changed everything. God's grace offers each of us the opportunity to enjoy an eternal relationship with God and He is restoring the brokenness in our hearts, relationships, and world. *Fourth,* today, because of God's love and sacrifice on our behalf, Christian camps provide the best available replica of God's original design. Christian camps, in a small way, mirror the Garden experience.

- Set in beautiful sites within God's creation.
- Profound opportunities for campers and guests to reconnect with God in deep and personal ways.
- Controlled environments where people find support and encouragement, where trust develops, and where the heavy burdens of life are shared.
- Opportunity for gift exploration and self-discovery allow campers and staff to align their lives with God's design.

Throughout the world, Christian camps' effectiveness is due in large part to the real-life experiences they provide. Campers, guests, and staff members take time away from the counterfeit world that merely poses as real. At camp they realign themselves more closely with God's magnificent intent.

*J*esus went up on a mountainside and called to him those he wanted, and they came to him. He appointed twelve--designating them apostles--that they might be with him and that he might send them out to preach and to have authority to drive out demons.

*Mark 3:13-15*

## Chapter Four
# Rhythm of Relationship
*Mark 3:13-15*

At its bare bones, boiled down, essential elements, Christianity has two parts: *first*, connecting with Jesus, and *second*, serving God. Without the life-giving *abiding with Jesus*, we lose our power, resources, and strength. But without our *service* to God, our lives are ineffective and fruitless. We need both. We need time with Jesus to revel in His mercy and to be refreshed by His grace. And we need opportunities to gratefully serve God by helping others and sharing the good news entrusted to us.

---

*We need time with Jesus to revel in His mercy and to be refreshed by His grace. And we need opportunities to gratefully serve God by helping others and sharing the good news entrusted to us.*

---

At first glance, Mark 3:13-15 seems like filler, a mere connecting statement to move the narrative from one thought to the next. But this short passage is much more than a simple transition. It captures the core of the Christian life and presents a foundational picture of the *rhythm of relationship* between us and God. And this rhythm is seen clearly and demonstrated specifically in Christian camping.

> *Jesus went up on a mountainside and called to him those he wanted, and they came to him. He appointed twelve--designating them apostles--that they might be with him and that he might send them out to preach and to have authority to drive out demons. (Mark 3:13-15)*

Mark's narrative captures these two fundamental aspects of the Christian life: spending time *with Jesus* and going out to *serve God*. Those two elements comprise the rhythm of the Christian life and the rhythm of Christian camping.

The disciples spent their lives traveling with Jesus, hiking, camping, eating, talking, listening, and learning. But at other times, they were sent out on assignments. Sometimes their activities were well-planned group endeavors; they ministered two-by-two. At other times were given individualized tasks – find a donkey, buy some food, or go fishing. They developed a pattern of spending time with Jesus, listening and learning. And then they were challenged to apply what they had learned. Their three year adventure with Jesus was a miniature picture of what was to come. Their earthly time with Jesus would end, and they would be called to *go and make disciples of all nations* (Matthew 28:19).

We see this challenge lived out by the disciples. Peter and John had been with Jesus more than three years, and people could tell. In Acts 4 they encountered a lame man who asked them for financial help; instead, they gave him what he needed more than a handout. They prayed and watched God provide him the ability to walk.

Despite this amazing act of power and mercy, not everyone was thrilled. This miracle of kindness enraged the religious establishment, and Peter and John were called to account for their actions. After their examination, the assessment of the religious leaders was telling. *When they saw the courage of Peter and John and realized that they were unschooled, ordinary men, they were astonished and they took note that these men had been with Jesus* (Acts 4:13).

The religious leaders laid down the law, forbidding Peter and John from further preaching. They even locked them in jail for the night. However, God had other plans. Overnight, God orchestrated a supernatural jailbreak and the next morning, they were back at the temple preaching the good news and helping those in need. The religious leaders were flabbergasted over the breakout and doubled down on their demand for the apostles to keep quiet about Jesus. Peter and John responded, *For we cannot help speaking about what we have seen and heard* (Acts 4:20).

*Before serving Christ, we must spend time with Christ*

Peter and John had spent time with Jesus, that was evident to the authorities. And they had a message about Jesus that they were compelled to share. That infuriated the authorities. Their pattern of life displayed that they had spent time with Jesus. And that time with Jesus compelled them to serve God and others. Both were crucial for Peter and John, and both are essential for us today.

## Being with Jesus

Being with Jesus comes first. Before serving Christ, we must spend time with Him. The demands of Christian camping can easily preempt our priorities and compromise our commitments. Jesus wants our hearts more than He wants our hands. Camp people tend to be doers, especially in America where accomplishment is key to our self-esteem, personal fulfilment, and self-satisfaction. For many of us, status is achieved through busyness, and success is measured through accumulation. But Jesus wants our hearts. Our work for Jesus should flow from a heart connected to Jesus in deep and personal ways.

Spending time with Jesus allows us to recharge our spiritual batteries and gives us the energy we need to serve Him. The challenge is to put one foot in front of the other in the faithful, steady routine of the Christian life. Too often we rely upon our own adrenalin to address big challenges and neglect to seek God's help in the routines of life. God's power however is what we need to faithfully confront life's big issues as well as the day-to-day drudgery. We need to spend time with Jesus to tap into the power that He provides.

Christian camps offer a wonderful setting for campers and guests to reengage with God in deep and personal ways. At camp, we are away from distractions, the demands of life, and the busyness that so easily seduces us. Camp settings provide the place for us to hit the refresh button, clear out extraneous elements, and reconnect with God. If campers and guests need those times, so do staff members.

---

*Spending time with Jesus gives us deeper insight into who He is so that we can strive to replicate – in a small way – His life in ours.*

---

Our connection with God can take many forms; an extended time of prayer beside a tranquil lake, meditation on a passage of scripture during a solitary hike, recommitting to trust and serve God while watching the embers of a dying campfire, or worshiping as the sunset emits magnificent rays of gold and grey. But these moments of connection need not be individual. Camp provides a platform for communities to pray together, reflect on scripture, encourage one another to walk with God, and as a grand choir, to praise God enthusiastically.

Spending time in God's presence is wonderful, refreshing, and life-giving. But those times of renewal are also inspiring and informative; they prepare us for what comes next. Spending time with Jesus provides the input we need to face challenges at home, work, school, and church with strength and confidence. Our special times of deep connection with God give us the strength to face intimidating obstacles and relentless attacks. Time with Jesus provides us the same strength and courage Peter and John employed to overcome their challenges.

Spending time with Jesus gives us deeper insight into who He is so that we can strive to replicate – in a small way – His life in ours. That is what *Christian* means – *little Christs*. We tend to assimilate the characteristics of those with whom we associate. **He who walks with the wise grows wise** (Proverbs 13:20). **Do not be misled: Bad company corrupts good character** (1 Corinthians 15:33). The more time we spend with Jesus, the greater the chances we will become *little Christs*, with godly wisdom and noble character. Christlikeness should be a priority for all who are serious about their faith.

In Matthew 22, Jesus confronts a group of religious leaders who tried to trap Him in a logical quagmire. They asked

Him about the Jewish responsibility to pay taxes to Caesar. Saying **yes** would alienate those who hated the Romans. Saying **no** would alienate those who tried to peacefully coexist. One response would put Him in trouble with the religious leaders, the other answer would put Him at odds with the political powers. A no-win situation for Jesus – or so they thought. As usual, Jesus was operating on a much higher plain. He examined a coin used to pay their taxes. Imprinted on the coin was a picture of Caesar, so Jesus said, *Give to Caesar what is Caesar's* (v. 21). But He didn't end there; He continued, *And to God what is God's* (v. 21). Caesar's image was on the coin, but God's image, ever so distorted, was stamped upon their hardened hearts – and ours.

God created each of us with His image and likeness etched on our hearts. We all struggle with the scars of sin and the disfigurement of our personal and corporate rebellion. Becoming increasingly Christlike transforms us more and more into our original design, back into alignment with the image of God.

Camp provides a place for those who desire to be more Christlike to connect with Jesus, and it sets aside time for campers to focus on their relationship with Him. The times of teaching, prayer, reflection, commitment, and rededication, both personal and communal, provide campers with intense, uninterrupted, focused connection points.

Camp also provides a wonderful context to learn ministry information and skills. The ability to study God's Word and communicate it effectively, along with the opportunity to learn hard work and effective ministry methods are woven into the fabric of camp for many campers and for all staff members.

---

 *We come to camp to be with Jesus so that we can go back home and make a difference for Jesus.*

---

## To Go Out

Being with Jesus is critical and wonderful, but it is only part of what God desires for us. After spending time with His disciples, Jesus sent them on a short-term mission trip. They went out to preach and engage in fierce spiritual warfare.

Some campers say they wish they could stay at camp forever, and that is a compliment all camp directors enjoy hearing. But it misses the point of camp. We come to camp to be *with Jesus* so that we can go back home and make a difference *for Jesus*. On the Mount of Transfiguration, Peter wanted to put up tents, stay a while, and extend the spiritual glow as long as possible. But camp is a temporary experience. We participate in camp so that we will be more effective in our relationships and responsibilities back at home, work, church, school, and community. Camp is a place to connect with God, but it is also a place of preparation for greater and more effective service.

Our faith grows as we spend time with Jesus, and a growing faith looks for opportunities to express itself. Even in the best of situations we still face testing and wrestle with doubt. Like the father who came to Jesus asking for help for his demon possessed son, we cry out, *I do believe; help me overcome my unbelief* (Mark 9:24). We gain confidence as we spend time with God and experience His supernatural strength and peace in our lives. As our relationship with Jesus grows, we gain the courage to engage the world with both truth and love.

Going out involves two elements; we saw them both in Peter and John's model in Acts 3. They relieved the suffering of the disabled man sitting by the temple and they also preached the Gospel. Neither is dispensable; they go hand in hand. We must address *physical* and *spiritual* needs. Our message rings hollow when we only preach and do nothing to resolve the suffering and pain of peoples' lives. And our message falls short if we work to resolve the physical needs of this life and fail to address spiritual issues that will ripple through eternity.

A camp setting provides opportunities to meet physical needs as well as spiritual needs. Jesus sends us out to do both, and He lets us practice at camp. Water safety, food service, special needs campers, horse safety, maintenance, medical procedures, and housekeeping are all ways to serve campers and meet physical needs. Bible studies, singing, devotions, campfires, one-on-one conversations, Bible memory and a host of other experiences provide opportunities to share the Gospel in word and deed.

*The rhythm of relationship involves times of deep encounter with God and times of active service for God.*

## Conclusion

Jesus describes two circumstances in which we should anticipate a special awareness of His presence. ***Once, where two or three come together in my name, there am I with them*** (Matthew 18:20). And another when He sends us out with the Great Commission. ***Go and make disciples ... and surely I am with you always, to the very end of the age*** (Matthew 28:19-20).

The rhythm of relationship involves times of deep encounter with God and times of active service for God. Both are essential. Camp enhances this rhythm; *first,* by coming together for times of worship, fellowship, and simple communion with Jesus, and *second,* by preparing us to return to our families, churches, jobs, schools, and communities ready and willing to serve Him more.

Some time later Paul said to Barnabas, "Let us go back and visit the brothers in all the towns where we preached the word of the Lord and see how they are doing." Barnabas wanted to take John, also called Mark, with them, but Paul did not think it wise to take him, because he had deserted them in Pamphylia and had not continued with them in the work.

*Acts 15:36-38*

Seated in a window was a young man named Eutychus, who was sinking into a deep sleep as Paul talked on and on. When he was sound asleep, he fell to the ground from the third story and was picked up dead. Paul went down, threw himself on the young man and put his arms around him. "Don't be alarmed," he said. "He's alive!"

*Acts 20:9-10*

Once when we were going to the place of prayer, we were met by a slave girl who had a spirit by which she predicted the future. She earned a great deal of money for her owners by fortune-telling. This girl followed Paul and the rest of us, shouting, "These men are servants of the Most High God, who are telling you the way to be saved." She kept this up for many days. Finally Paul became so troubled that he turned around and said to the spirit, "In the name of Jesus Christ I command you to come out of her!" At that moment the spirit left her.

*Acts 16:16-18*

### Chapter Five
# Three Campers in Acts[4]
*The Book of Acts*

All campers arrive with luggage. Maybe a small overnight bag or possibly a back-breaking footlocker, but they all bring something. And that is just the baggage we can see. Many carry heavy loads of mistakes, questions, loss, disappointment, or abuse with them to camp. Sometimes those bags return home unopened, and sometimes they are left at the foot of the cross.

Looking deeper, we find three types of unseen luggage. The *first* is filled with selfish interests, immature choices, ineffective image management tools, fear, and arrogance. A *second* contains unanswered questions, doubts, and unresolved tensions. What is true? What provides meaning? What is best? And what path should I follow in the days ahead? The *third* and heaviest is filled with deep hurt, abuse, and unspeakable pain. Their bags are packed with sins of others and their own. These festering wounds may remain packed away, but they will always be tender to the touch. Camp provides a place for healing to occur and God, the Great Physician, to start the curative process.

No one-size ministry fits every camper's unique circumstance; however, wise camping leaders ask themselves which type of baggage each camper is bringing to camp and adjust accordingly. Millions of campers attend Christian camps each year in the United States and around the world. A trio of young people in the book of Acts personify three basic categories of campers and the hidden luggage they carry.

## *John Mark – The Good Sunday School Boy*

Let me skip to the end of the story, John Mark turns out to be a great man of God; he just needed a little extra time and attention to get where God wanted him to be. In the last chapter of Paul's final letter, he recognizes that Mark's ministry value had risen significantly over the years. He tells Timothy, **Only Luke is with me. Get Mark and bring him with you, because he is helpful to me in my ministry** (2 Timothy 4:11). Mark also went on to write one of the four primary accounts of Jesus' life, the Gospel of Mark. Many believe Mark's story about Jesus was heavily influenced by Peter and provides many firsthand accounts of monumental events. So, despite some wrong turns and the need for a few *mulligans* along the way, he turned out well. Even though Mark carried some baggage with him, God was always redeeming his story. And what God did 2,000 years ago He still does for campers today.

In Acts 12, we find ourselves in Mark's home when Peter was miraculously delivered from prison. Peter made his way from the jail to the house belonging to John Mark's mother. *When this had dawned on him, he went to the house of Mary the mother of John, also called Mark, where many people had gathered and were praying* (Acts 12:12). Apparently, Mark's parents were leaders in the early Church and their home was a common meeting place. The house must have been fairly large indicating that the family had some financial resources as well.

Colossians 4:10 tells us that Barnabas, one of the most prominent leaders of the early Church, was John Mark's cousin. And Barnabas made a sizable gift to the Church, again showing that the family probably had above average financial reserves (Acts 4:36-37).

So, when Barnabas and Paul set out on their first missionary journey, they picked John Mark to go along as their helper. Why not? He looked like a good kid from a fine Christian family. *The two of them, sent on their way by the Holy Spirit, went down to Seleucia and sailed from there to Cyprus. When they arrived at Salamis, they proclaimed the word of God in the Jewish synagogues. John was with them as their helper* (Acts 13:4-5).

What a great opportunity for young John Mark! But alas, he only lasted eight verses. After a confrontational encounter with a sorcerer and a politician, John Mark was done and headed home. *From Paphos, Paul and his com-*

*panions sailed to Perga in Pamphylia, where John left them to return to Jerusalem* (Acts 13:13). We don't know why John Mark abandoned his duties. Maybe because of the heated, public conflict. Some think he was homesick; others speculate he was upset with Paul's leadership; others conjecture that theology played a part in the separation. Who knows? All we know is that when circumstances turned against him, he left.

---

*John Mark needed the accountability of Paul and the encouragement of Barnabas. But mostly he needed a personal commitment and connection to God that would sustain him when times became tough. And so do millions of campers today!*

---

After a remarkable missionary journey, Paul and Barnabas returned home and shared their stories with the Church at Jerusalem. Then they made plans for their next missionary adventure.

*Some time later Paul said to Barnabas, "Let us go back and visit the brothers in all the towns where we preached the word of the Lord and see how they are doing." Barnabas wanted to take John, also called Mark, with them, but Paul did not think it wise to take him, because he*

*had deserted them in Pamphylia and had not contin-
ued with them in the work. They had such a sharp disagreement that they parted company. Barnabas took
Mark and sailed for Cyprus, but Paul chose Silas and
left, commended by the brothers to the grace of the
Lord. He went through Syria and Cilicia, strengthening
the churches. (Acts 15:36-41)*

Paul was not about to put the mission at risk with another immature response to difficulty. At the same time,
Barnabas was determined not to abandon a young man
who showed so much promise. John Mark needed to grow
up. Paul and Barnabas parted company. Paul took a new
team and headed north toward Turkey and then on to
Greece. Barnabas took John Mark and headed back to
Cyprus, the exact place where John Mark had failed. This
provided John Mark an opportunity for a fresh start and
the second chance that would reshape his life.

John Mark was a good kid who grew up in a good home
with spiritual leaders for parents. He lived in a context
where Christianity was assumed and in a family that cen-
tered its life on Christ and His Church. But he was living on
*last-name* faith, not *first-name faith*. The faith of his mother
and father were the props that held him up spiritually,
but when they were gone, so was the spiritual strength he
needed to endure.

John Mark needed the *accountability* of Paul and the *encouragement* of Barnabas. But mostly he needed a personal commitment and connection to God that would sustain him when times became tough. And so do millions of campers today!

---

*John Mark needed the accountability of Paul and the encouragement of Barnabas. But mostly he needed a personal commitment and connection to God that would sustain him when times became tough. And so do millions of campers today!*

---

## Eutychus – The Boy in the Window

Next, we meet Eutychus, a young man whose life was being pulled in different directions. Paul's stay in Troas was brief, so he scheduled a late-night preaching service in a three-story house. A curious young man attended and found a perch in a top-story window.

*On the first day of the week we came together to break bread. Paul spoke to the people and, because he intended to leave the next day, kept on talking until midnight. There were many lamps in the upstairs room where we were*

*meeting. Seated in a window was a young man named*
*Eutychus. (Acts 20:7-9a)*

From his unique vantage point, Eutychus could listen
to Paul while at the same time watch the activity in the
streets below. From his perch, he may have watched other
children playing and talking; observed street vendors selling
their wares and shoppers hurrying home with their goods.
Perhaps pretty girls walked by. Friends might have waved
for him to come and join them. Where he sat, the voices of
the world could whisper in one ear while the message of
the Gospel rang in the other.

Like Eutychus, many campers today are caught in the
middle. The Gospel message is presented clearly and powerfully, yet the seductive messages of the world are calling
as well. Ethical questions, moral choices, and intellectual
challenges pull our campers toward precarious precipices,
placing this generation in grave danger.

All the while, Paul droned on. Don't get me wrong, Paul
was preaching wonderful content! This was pure, unfiltered,
crystal-clear Gospel. Paul taught his heart out and presented
powerful truth. But he was putting Eutychus to sleep.

*(Eutychus) was sinking into a deep sleep as Paul talked*
*on and on. When he was sound asleep, he fell to the*
*ground from the third story and was picked up dead.*
*Paul went down, threw himself on the young man and*

*put his arms around him. "Don't be alarmed," he said. "He's alive!" (Acts 20:9-10)*

The things of the world enticed him, but the ministry style Paul employed didn't help. In fact, it contributed to his *downfall!* The unintended consequence of Paul's teaching style was Eutychus' three-story fall to his death. The meeting recessed abruptly as the people raced downstairs to help the young man. But they were too late.

 *Powerful content and personal connections converge at camp to create life-changing, transformational moments.*

When Paul arrived at the scene of the tragedy, he threw himself upon Eutychus, wrapping his arms around the dead boy's body. In that moment, his life returned, and he was saved.

The Gospel message was unaltered, but Paul's ministry method changed radically. The preaching presentation, at least for Eutychus, was at best ineffective and at worst deadly. It was not until Paul got close to him and wrapped his arms around him, that Eutychus' life was restored.

Christian camps provide a magnificent context to combine these two crucial ministry styles. They create settings for the proclamation of the Gospel with strength and clarity, but they also establish opportunities for mature believers to engage campers with relational connections and personal encounters. Powerful *content* and personal *connections* converge at camp to create life-changing, transformational moments.

## Libby – The Enslaved/Liberated Girl

Finally, we encounter a little girl caught in the clutches of first-century traffickers, I call her Libby – Liberated Libby.

This young girl was enslaved twice – once by the demonic spirits that controlled her very existence and second by the exploitive men who used her for their financial gain.

> *Once when we were going to the place of prayer, we were met by a slave girl who had a spirit by which she predicted the future. She earned a great deal of money for her owners by fortune-telling (Acts 16:16).*

She was powerless, in bondage, and a victim of those who used cruel, selfish control to rule over her. The demonic forces enabled her to function as a fortune teller, and her owners charged handsomely for her services. Evil spirits, evil owners, and evil clients all took advantage of her vulnerable state.

Meanwhile, Paul had assembled the *dream team*. With him in Philippi were Luke, Silas, and Timothy. Seeking to plant a new church in this thriving Macedonian city, they preached, taught, made contacts, and prayed.

Each afternoon these Christian leaders dedicated themselves to prayer in a special location, and their pathway took them near the little enslaved girl and her exploitive owners. As this band of spiritual giants passed, she chided them, sarcastically announcing their arrival. *These are the servants of the Most-High God, who are telling you the way to be saved* (v. 17). She was right in her description, but terribly wrong in her attitude.

Paul and the others tried to ignore her; for many days they pretended to not hear her jeering comments and derisive catcalls. They walked past unfazed. But they could take her taunting only so long. Luke records his first-hand account. *She kept this up for many days. Finally, Paul became so troubled that he turned and said to the spirit, "In the name of Jesus Christ I command you to come out of her!" At that moment the spirit left her* (v. 18).

Maybe for the wrong reasons but certainly with the right outcome, the miraculous liberation process began. The demonic spirits were no match for the power of God; they lost their grip on her life. The human owners were no longer able to profit from her fortune telling services. They lost their income, and the clients who depended on her advice lost their insider information. Enraged people sought Paul and his friends to vent their anger and extract their revenge, and they did!

A riot broke out. Paul and Silas were arrested, beaten, thrown in prison, closely guarded, and placed in stocks

(Acts 16:19-24). Yet at midnight, Paul and Silas were singing songs of praise to God. They had seen God liberate a young girl from the power of sin, and no pain or imprisonment could keep them from singing.

---

*The acceptance they desire leads down the rabbit hole of dark fantasy, leaving them in the dangerous grip of despair.*

---

Regrettably, more and more young people are becoming enslaved to the evil that abounds in this world. Sex, drugs, alcohol, occult, gangs, violence, and online decadence become places of distraction and refuge for many young people. The security they seek soon becomes a new form of slavery. The acceptance they desire leads down the rabbit hole of dark fantasy, leaving them in the dangerous grip of despair.

Thankfully, some of them show up at camp. A few want to be there; many are forced to attend by their parents or caregivers. The chips on their shoulders are surpassed only by the pain in their hearts. These campers are easy to ignore or at least avoid. The safe thing is to walk away. Getting too involved will be messy and painful. But kids like Libby need the Gospel as much as the John Marks and the Eutyches. And camp provides a great setting to share the truth and love of God with those who needed it most.

*Camp provides a great setting to share the truth and love of God with those who need it the most.*

We don't have any details about Libby's life after this encounter, but we do know that God had set her free. And we know that thousands of campers arrive each summer with bags filled with pain, abuse, and exploitation, and they need spiritual liberation as well.

## Conclusion

Camp ministry is challenging. Campers arrive carrying all sorts of baggage. Whether it's a regular kid from a church-going home who needs accountability and encouragement, a camper with deep questions, needing truth and love, or a troubled young person desperately needing freedom and hope, they can all find good news at the cross of Christ. The Gospel is alive and well and presented each day at Christian camps around the world.

Camp is a great place for young people to release the immaturity, questions, and rebellion of life, and refill their hearts with God's love, joy, peace, and so much more!

*U*nless the Lord builds the house,
    the builders labor in vain.
Unless the Lord watches over the city,
    the guards stand watch in vain.

² *In vain you rise early*
    *and stay up late,*
*toiling for food to eat—*
    *for he grants sleep to those he loves.*

³ *Children are a heritage from the Lord,*
    *offspring a reward from him.*
⁴ *Like arrows in the hands of a warrior*
    *are children born in one's youth.*

⁵ *Blessed is the man*
    *whose quiver is full of them.*
*They will not be put to shame*
    *when they contend with their*
    *opponents in court.*

Psalm 127
*A song of ascents. Of Solomon.*

### Chapter Six
# Family Camp
*Psalm 127*

I rarely read a book's introduction; I just jump in and get some pages behind me. But often, the introduction is vital to understanding the author's perspective or argument and sometimes it sheds light on important aspects of the writing. The superscriptions introducing many psalms also seem like wasted space. What is a *Maskil*? What or who is *Mahalath Leannoth*? And who was *Asaph*? But for Psalm 127, these introductory comments are significant. The notation, *A Psalm of Ascent*, indicates that this song was to be sung by pilgrims ascending Mount Zion as they approached Jerusalem during each of the three great national festivals. These songs prepared the people's hearts and minds. They were designed to help the travelers set aside the distractions they were leaving behind and prepare them to fully engage the events that lay ahead.

The second notation indicates that Solomon, the wisest person who ever lived, penned these words. But he was not an ivory-tower wise man; he was a consummate builder and dominant leader. He reigned over a huge empire while building a massive palace, magnificent temple, powerful army, immeasurable treasury, and unrivaled harem.

These two points in the superscription to the Psalm provide significant and relevant information to help us explore this insightful psalm that addresses the heart of family camping.

Imagine a man during biblical times with a wife and a house full of small children. He owns a leather shop and business is good, maybe too good. He is backed up with orders for sandals, harnesses, aprons, and belts. Several fresh hides have arrived, and he has nowhere to store them. As if that were not enough, he is in the midst of adding a new room to his shop so that he can hire additional workers. Building his business is overwhelming, and he is always watchful of competitors who may steal his customers.

He comes home from a long day at work and is met by the excited jabber of his children, *Only one more week until we go to Jerusalem!* they cry.

*Oh, maybe not this time,* says the weary father. He glances toward his wife and sees the disappointment in her eyes. *It's just that I have so much to do at work – the building, the orders, the new hides!*

*I know,* says his wife, *but the children have been looking forward to it, and you need a break.*

He looks at his dinner and the sad faces around him at the table. *Okay, we'll go. But only if I get caught up on my orders and get the new addition to the shop weathered in.*

The children are excited, and mother is relieved. Only dad feels overwhelmed.

The week passes and projects are crossed off the list. The additional room is not completed but it is secure and weather tight. The hides are stored under the workbench, and off they go to Jerusalem.

While hiking the dusty country roads, they are joined by other pilgrims also coming to celebrate and worship. His children are running hither and yon; his wife is talking excitedly with strangers, but dad's mind is back at work. He fumes about the things at home, undone and unprotected. He has just walked away from his major building project and left vulnerable his livelihood and all his worldly possessions.

Then, from the back of the line comes singing. The words are familiar; they are sung every year.

*Unless the Lord builds the house,*
    *the builders labor in vain.*
      *Unless the Lord watches over the city,*
        *the guards stand watch in vain.*
*[2] In vain you rise early and stay up late,*
      *toiling for food to eat—*
*for he grants sleep to those he loves.*
*(Psalm 127:1-2)*

*Many decisions simply come down to our true priorities. Do we want to keep building and protecting our work and business or do we want to invest in the next generation?*

Dad mulls the words over in his mind. God is the ultimate builder and protector. *He will take care of my addition and watch over my supplies while I'm away.* He feels better and begins to relax in God's protective care.

Then the second verse begins. The words are more meaningful and pointed than in previous years. His children are growing up so quickly.

> ³ *Children are a heritage from the Lord,*
>     *offspring a reward from him.*
> ⁴ *Like arrows in the hands of a warrior*
>     *are children born in one's youth.*
> ⁵ *Blessed is the man*
>     *whose quiver is full of them.*
> *They will not be put to shame*
>     *when they contend with their*
>     *opponents in court.*
>         *(Psalm 127:3-5)*

His focus shifts from his work to his family. *Yes, this is good; my children are playing, laughing, singing, and running.*

He is delighted to have time to reconnect with them as they make their way toward Jerusalem.

Today, families miss attending family camp for many reasons, some very legitimate: finances, work schedules, or family responsibilities. But many decisions simply come down to our true priorities. Do we want to keep building and protecting our work and business or do we want to invest in the next generation? Like many good things in life, responsibility can become an idol. When we cannot walk away and trust God to sustain and protect, we have lost

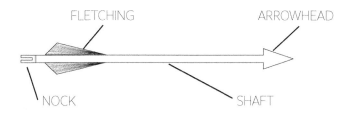

sight of the bigger picture. We need to hum a few verses from Psalm 127 and regain perspective.

The lyrics, *like arrows in the hands of a warrior*, rolls over and over in the mind of the father in our story. Four thoughts emerge. *First*, the delicate fletching. How often has he crushed the tender emotions of his children? He needs opportunities to laugh, sing, rejoice, wonder, and perhaps cry with his children. These shared emotional moments provide models of appropriate responses to pleasures, pressures, and pains of life. A healthy emotional fletching would provide the guidance his children need to keep flying on course.

But so much caution is also needed to protect against harsh words, critical glances, or over-reactions that could damage the delicate emotions under his care. It is good to refocus on this relentless and precious responsibility.

---

 *The parent-child connection takes time to develop. It requires conversations – sometimes about nothing, sometimes about serious life issues. And parents seldom know when the discussion might dive deep.*

---

*Second*, the straight strong shaft. Each of his children needs to develop the strong shaft of trustworthy character, moral integrity, and tenacious focus. As they walk toward Jerusalem, he studies their responses and choices. He wonders what lessons each needs to learn to become stronger and straighter to face the days ahead. He formulates plans for the healthy development of each child.

*Third,* the arrowhead. How will these children make an impact in the future without sharpened skills? What skills will they need to manage their money, organize projects, prioritize their time, and interact with others? What can I do as a father to help them make the greatest impact in the years ahead? What needs sharpening, and how can I help?

*Fourth,* he muses on the nock. The tiny connection point at the end of the arrow is critical if the power of the bow is to be transferred to the arrow. Without the small but critical connection, the arrow will never benefit from the strength of the bow. The parent-child connection takes time to develop. It requires conversations – sometimes about nothing, sometimes about serious life issues. And parents seldom know when the discussion might dive deep. He realizes that his kids need hugs. Healthy, appropriate touch helps solidify the connection. Maybe the most significant connections come when eyes meet, and parents and children's souls connect.

Family camp, like the walk to Jerusalem, provides a place where parents and children can connect deeply. Camp is not the only place where these connections can occur, but it is a significant opportunity. The emotional care, character development, skill enhancement, and deep life-long bonding flow naturally and accelerate at family camp.

---

*Wise parents periodically set aside the things they are building and protecting and invest deeply in their families.*

---

## And Then They're Off

The trajectory of our children is not always what we want nor their destination what we desired. Forces beyond our control can blow any arrow off course. But most often, the way they start determines the way they finish.

The image of the arrow could be connected to that of a hunter or a target shooter, but Solomon chooses a warrior. There is a battle raging for the hearts and minds of the next generation. Parents must be warriors for their children, fighting for their physical, emotional, and spiritual well-being.

The fight is not to ensure that the child will live a safe and comfortable life, rather that the child will grow up to become a noble warrior as well. Solomon goes on, ***They will contend with their enemies in the gate*** (v. 5). In Solomon's time, the city gate was the town hall, financial hub, real estate office, and newsroom. It was where things happened in their culture. Well-prepared children – many who go with their parents to family camp – will be the ones shaping the culture and values of the next generation.

For parents, the days go slow, but the years go fast. Children are born – and then they are gone. Like the father who almost skipped Camp Jerusalem to build his leather shop and protect his new hides, we all have choices to make and priorities to set. Wise parents periodically set aside the things they are building and protecting and invest deeply in their families.

## *Conclusion*

We hear much today about sustainability. I have no doubt that Solomon, the wisest man who ever lived, had plans for his kingdom to remain powerful and secure for years and years after he departed this life. The army, economy, and infrastructure were all secure, but his son, Rehoboam was not. Within a few weeks after his death, everything Solomon had built and protected was demolished. The one critical element he neglected to build and protect was his son. Rehoboam failed his first and most significant leadership test bringing to naught all his father had spent his life building and protecting.

---

*Family camp provides the breaks we need to get away for an extended time to enjoy God's creation, invest in relationships, realign ourselves with God, and refocus on what is truly important in our lives. And it allows us to prepare the next generation for the challenges ahead.*

---

Sustainability may or may not be a noble endeavor, but the only thing that will remain for long are the lives we influence today. Solomon knew the importance of investing in his children, but he lacked follow through. He was too busy building his capital, fortune, army, and harem. And he was distracted by protecting his empire economically and militarily. All the while neglecting to train and prepare his son for the challenges ahead.

Family camp provides the breaks we need to get away for an extended time to enjoy God's creation, invest in relationships, realign ourselves with God, and refocus on what is truly important in our lives. And it allows us to prepare the next generation for the challenges ahead.

*I*n those days when the number of disciples was increasing, the Hellenistic Jews among them complained against the Hebraic Jews because their widows were being overlooked in the daily distribution of food. ²So the Twelve gathered all the disciples together and said, "It would not be right for us to neglect the ministry of the word of God in order to wait on tables. ³Brothers and sisters, choose seven men from among you who are known to be full of the Spirit and wisdom. We will turn this responsibility over to them ⁴ and will give our attention to prayer and the ministry of the word."

⁵This proposal pleased the whole group. They chose Stephen, a man full of faith and of the Holy Spirit; also Philip, Procorus, Nicanor, Timon, Parmenas, and Nicolas from Antioch, a convert to Judaism. ⁶They presented these men to the apostles, who prayed and laid their hands on them.

⁷So the word of God spread. The number of disciples in Jerusalem increased rapidly, and a large number of priests became obedient to the faith.

*Acts 6:1-7*

## Chapter Seven
# The Complexity of Camp
*Acts 6:1-7*

Looks can be deceiving! A gymnast tumbling gracefully across the floor, figure skaters ice dancing, a pastry chef baking a pie, or a composer writing a song – how tough could those things be? Well, just try them!

Tasks that appear simple and easy to perform can actually be complex and extremely difficult. Christian camping is one of those challenges. The casual observer wonders, what does it take to be a camp director besides a whistle and a clipboard? But once engaged in leadership at a Christian camp, the challenge to perform well can be daunting.

The wide variety of camp responsibilities generates the complexity. Leading a Christian camp involves serving hundreds (if not thousands) of meals every day, keeping sewers unclogged, speaking in chapel, cleaning the swimming pool, appreciating donors, fixing computers, filing government reports, evaluating staff members, informing board members, and so much more.

For a major corporation to be successful it merely needs to show a profit – the bigger the better. But camps have a much greater challenge; they must succeed in multiple areas. This complexity contributes to the trauma and drama of camp ministry. The multifaceted challenge requires each Christian camp to succeed in at least three critical realms: *first,* as an effective ministry; *second,* as a healthy community; and *third,* as a well-managed organization. Failure in any one of these three essential arenas will result in failure for all. Success is only achieved when all three areas are coordinated well through strong leadership and effective management.

Succeeding in all these areas would be tough in any setting, but the problem is exacerbated when operating on a tight budget, lacking skilled staff (paid or unpaid), and often running out of beds, meeting rooms, and dining space. When resources are scarce, people become protective of their turf and strive to defend what they have. Self-centered responses can multiply the complexity and lead to greater challenges.

## Complexity in the Early Church

Ministry, community, and organizational activities converge in Acts 6:1-7 and the complexity of running a church or camp is played out in high definition. In this brief story we discover the challenge of succeeding in all three arenas and the threat that accompanies failure in any of them.

THE COMPLEXITY OF CAMP

The story in Acts begins on a high note, *In those days when the number of disciples was increasing*. (v. 6:1a). These were good times. Thousands of people were turning to Christ and the number of believers was increasing significantly. This growth, however, stretched their available resources and strained relationships. In their case, the limited resource was food. The Grecian Jews among them complained against the Hebraic Jews because their widows were being overlooked in the daily distribution of food (v. 6:1b).

The Apostles faced the three-layered challenge of sustaining a meaningful ministry, maintaining unity within the body of believers, and operating effectively with the limited resources available to them. Let's look at how they responded to this complex and treacherous set of challenges.

## Effective Ministry

Two of the major ministry themes that emerge in the first five chapters of Acts are *prayer* and *preaching*. Prayer was central to the life of the early Church. They gathered for times of prayer and praise (Acts 2:47), and to voice mutual concerns to the Lord (Acts 4:24). When Peter and others were arrested, the Church responded with a prayer meeting. When they prayed, God listened and responded. *After they prayed, the place where they were meeting was shaken* (Acts 4:31). The earthquake provided a physical manifestation of God's power and protection in response to their prayers. The commitment to fervent prayer was essential in the life of the early Church.

The early Church was also committed to studying and sharing God's Word. Peter and the other apostles preached on Pentecost and 3,000 were converted (Acts 2:41). When a crowd gathered to witness a lame man's healing and his joyful leaping throughout the temple area, Peter and John used the opportunity to preach the good news (Acts 3:8-12). Another 5,000 responded due to that presentation of the Gospel (Acts 4:4). When threatened by the local authorities, Peter and John responded that they could do nothing other than proclaim what they had seen and heard (Acts 4:20). Ultimately, several apostles were imprisoned for preaching but when an angel enabled their escape, they returned to the temple area the next day and continued to proclaim their message. Beaten for their efforts, they rejoiced that they were worthy of suffering for Christ (Acts 5:40-42).

## Community Unity

Unity within the family of believers was highly valued by the early Church. When else in the history of the Church could it be said that *All the believers were one in heart and mind* (Acts 4:32)? They shared all their possessions, provided for the needy, and ate meals together (Acts 2:44-

46). Understandably, many of these early disciples expected Christ to return any day, so there was no need to protect their retirement funds. They faced immense opportunities and intense needs and time was short, so personal wellbeing was sacrificed for the good of all. The result was that *Every day they continued to meet together in the temple courts. They broke bread in their homes and ate together with glad and sincere hearts* (Acts 2:46). They devoted themselves to the apostles' teaching and to the fellowship, to the breaking of bread and to prayer (Acts 2:42). Unity was strong and evidenced by their profound sacrifices for one another.

## Operating Effectiveness

Strategic leadership and effective management were needed to ensure that the Church succeeded as an organization. Responsible operational practices required them to wisely manage their limited resources. They needed to make good personnel decisions, communicate effectively, set priorities, and delegate authority. The Apostles had multiple objectives. They needed to address the presenting problem of a limited food supply, but they also needed to avert the potential division between two primary groups within the body. All the while, they needed to remain focused on their mission. To accomplish these three objectives the disciples employed several universal leadership and management practices.

Before we explore the principles and techniques of leading and managing well, let's talks about the elephant in the room. Sympathetic yet patronizing friends from the business world often wonder (sometimes to themselves and sometimes aloud), *why can't this camp be run like a business?* The answer becomes obvious, once ministry leaders rebound from the initial intimidation of the question. For starters – because a Christian camp is not a business – no ministry is. Why should something that is not a business act like a business?

The business world does not own the universal principles and behavioral laws of management and leadership. But they have applied them very well. So well, in fact, that we think that those universal organizational principles are the property of the business community. Camps should employ effective leadership and management practices, but that is very different from *being a business*. Camps, churches, and all non-profit charities exist for different purposes than businesses. Why not run like a business? Because camps exist to impact lives, not to make a profit. That is a noticeably big difference.

Peter Drucker, a guru in the world of business and management, defines well the role and identity of the non-profit world. Drucker says,

*They (non-profits) do something very different from either business or government. Business supplies either goods or services. Government controls. A business has discharged its task when the customer buys the product, pays for it, and is satisfied with it. Government has discharged its function when its policies are effective. The "non-profit" institution neither supplies goods or services nor controls. Its product is neither a pair of shoes or an effective regulation. Its product is a changed human being.[5]*

Camps, churches, and other non-profit ministries may provide food, lodging, and recreation, and sell a few T-shirts. Yes, those are goods and services, but they are items provided to campers for a very different intent than to make a profit. At times, goods and services help set the stage for camp ministries, but to operate effectively. They are means for seeing God work in people's hearts and to change lives for eternity.

---

*Every part of our camp ministries should be led and managed well. But a well-managed ministry is different from a well-managed business.*

---

We often mistake leadership and management activity for **business** practices or see them as tools flowing from

the **business community**. However, leadership and management are common tools available to business, ministry, and
government institutions. Every part of our camp ministries
should be led and managed well. But a well-managed ministry is different from a well-managed business. Business
is not the fountainhead of wise leadership or effective
management. The business community has been highly
successful in understanding and utilizing leadership and
management principles. Generally, they have applied these
tools more effectively than ministries, non-profits, educational institutions, or governments. But the business world
does not own the leadership or management arena.

*While the Apostles struggled to maintain the
unity within the community, they were deeply
committed to avoiding mission drift and to sustaining their core ministry of prayer and preaching.*

For camps to prosper they need to succeed as organizations in the sense that they utilize leadership and
management practices well and strive to be exceptionally
well run. A financial surplus is only significant if lives are
being transformed for God's glory.

To ensure that the *ministry thing* remains the *main
thing*, camps must make certain that they are not distracted

from their call to ministry and that their community is not divided.

## The Dual Threats – Division and Distraction

Within the healthy, growing, unified, ministry-minded, smooth operating context of the early Church, the dark and dangerous twin threats of *division* and *distraction* emerged. The Apostles were called upon to address both challenges and to protect the fledgling Church from both potential hazards. While the Apostles struggled to maintain the unity within the community, they were deeply committed to avoiding mission drift and to sustaining their core ministry of *prayer* and *preaching*.

Division was a real threat. The Jewish community in Jerusalem had two distinct elements: Hebraic Jews and Grecian Jews. The Hebraic Jews were locals. They grew up in the area, understood the culture, and knew how the systems worked. The Grecian Jews, however, were not so fortunate. They had returned to Jerusalem after being raised in other parts of the Mediterranean world. Their heritage was Jewish, but their cultural perspectives had been shaped by Greek and Roman influences. And they certainly did not know about the side entrance to the food pantry. When the food supply ran low, the Hebraic Jews stayed well-fed but the Grecian Jews were moved to the back of the line. This injustice did not sit well with the newcomers.

This ominous threat of *division* within the Church community could have led to a second and possibly more perilous problem - *distraction*. The leaders' attention had been focused on their mission. Their unique roles and responsibilities within the newly formed Church were directed entirely toward the spiritual aspects of the ministry—prayer and biblical preaching. But they also knew that the fledgling Church was facing a very divisive problem with potentially explosive consequences. This drama of food distribution needed to be addressed but not at the expense of their calling. So how to respond? How could they resolve the tensions within the body and sustain their prayer and preaching ministries?

## The Leadership and Management Solutions

Let's see how these wise and effective leaders and managers applied godly principles and practices in Acts 6 to solve a thorny and complex problem. Perhaps camps today can benefit from their model.

Any picture of ministry in Acts forces us to ask, is this a *picture* of what ministry looked like then, or a *model* for how ministry should happen today? The answer is, *yes* and *no*. There are cultural and practical realities that shape the context within which the Apostles worked. Their circumstances were different from ours and we need to recognize those distinctions. However, we can learn much from the excellent and effective practices they employed that transcend time and location. These examples can help us deal with the complex challenges of leading and managing camp ministries in our world today.

What happens first is of utmost importance, and the Apostles made the right move responding directly and quickly. *So the Twelve gathered all the disciples together and said, "It would not be right for us to neglect the ministry of the word of God in order to wait on tables..."* (Acts 6:2). Several principles emerge in this passage but none greater than the *significance and centrality of the mission*. The Apostles were laser focused on fulfilling the ministry of prayer and preaching that had been entrusted to them.

Several universal principles were applied 2,000 years ago to save the early Church, and they can be applied today to help maintain the organizational, relational, and spiritual health of camp ministries.

### Limited Resource Management.

We live in a world of limited resources; that is part of being finite people. Limited resources are often the source of divisions. Whether it is lack of money, volunteers, classroom space, water skiing time, sleeping bags, white horses, or top bunks, limited resources make us selfish. Within our camps there is only so much money. And the maintenance staff desperately needs a bigger tractor, the food service department is crying for a new oven, and the program director cannot go one more summer without a climbing wall. As in the early Church, none of us is opposed to others having their needs met as long as our needs are satisfied first.

We all need to recognize that this world's resources are limited. There is only so much time and money available, and only so many volunteers to go around. If we only look at these from our one-sided perspectives, we will allow the small divisions of self-interest to grow. Budgets allocate limited money, schedules plan the use of limited time, and organizational charts distribute the ministry's limited staff and volunteers. We all need to see and honor the overarching goals and objectives of the ministry.

### Open Communication.

Open communication is critical to addressing and overcoming the initial stages of division and it is essential for developing and deepening trust. When the difference of opinion came to the Apostles' attention, they did not shirk their responsibility, deny the reality of the problem, or hope things would get better all on their own. They initiated an open meeting to address the problem with grace and candor. They recognized the danger of this disagreement and the potentially destructive nature of the problem. The early Church in Jerusalem understood that listening to the various perspectives, providing an open, grace-filled forum in which to air opinions, and allowing a plan of action to emerge would unify the group and surface people willing to help resolve the crisis. Open, grace-filled communication is a practice that great leaders and effective managers employ today.

### Priority Setting.

Setting priorities simply means that the organization understands and articulates what is important relative to everything else. Priorities allow an organization to say *no* to good - yet unrelated ideas. Maintaining well-articulated priorities allows the institutions to focus all their available resources toward achieving desired objectives. Well-established priorities permit the organization to align its limited human and material resources toward achieving established goals.

---

*The early Church in Jerusalem understood that listening to the various perspectives, providing an open, grace-filled forum in which to air opinions, and allowing a plan of action to emerge would unify the group and surface people willing to help resolve the crisis.*

---

The Apostles knew that their responsibilities were to pray and preach. Those activities had been central in the first five chapters and the Church had prospered remarkably. Prayer exemplified the Apostles' desire to stay close and connected to God Himself. Preaching demonstrated their desire to reach out to others and see lives changed. They were committed to following these priorities and unwilling to let anything, even the good work of equitably feeding hungry people, stand in their way. They wanted to resolve the source of potential division, but they were unwilling to allow any *good thing* to distract them from pursuing the *best things*.

---

 *Delegating ensures that important tasks are accomplished by the right people.*

---

### Delegation.

The Apostles delegated the important yet potentially distracting work of food distribution (waiting tables) to others. The group of seven leaders who were selected to address this problem all had Greek names. As leaders of the Hellenistic Jews, this group was deeply and personally concerned to find a resolution for this problem. Delegating is not about a leader avoiding things he or she does not want to do and giving bad jobs to someone else. Delegating ensures that important tasks are accomplished by the right people. Delegating recognizes that no one can do it all and that a key leader's limited resources of time, energy, and abilities must be focused on the things that they do best or that can only be done by the person in their position.

At the same time, others should be deputized to address related challenges contributing to the success of the entire organization.

*Position Profiles.* Delegating is not a capricious, random act. Extreme care should be given to selecting the right person for the right job. This begins with a position profile. In the case of the early Church in this passage, two criteria were critical to success in this sensitive role and the Apostles were uncompromising. Both *professional skill* and *spiritual depth* were needed, and these two essential qualities guided the selection process. The Apostles' delegation procedure provided clear guidelines but allowed the whole group to make the selection. The Apostles said, **Brothers, choose seven men from among you who are known to be full of the Spirit and wisdom. We will turn this responsibility over to them** (v. 6:3). The position profile was clear; *first,* they were to be full of God's Spirit, and *second,* full of wisdom. They were to be exemplary in their spiritual lives and highly skilled in their professional responsibilities.

*Empowerment.* Once the selection process was complete, the Apostles did not walk away and abandon the Seven to work in a vacuum. They demonstrated their support and empowered these new recruits to do their job. Luke's account says, **They presented these men to the Apostles, who prayed and laid their hands on them** (v. 6:6). The Apostles were committed to prayer, so they did what they did best - they prayed. The disciples commissioned the newly appointed workers to their ministry by laying hands on them. Fulfilling this task was not a nuisance; it was an extension of the Apostles' hearts. Empowering those to whom the work was delegated allowed the Apostles to focus and fulfill their ministry responsibilities of prayer and preaching as well as honor their commitment to retain unity within the body.

---

 *The dual dangers of division and distraction were thwarted through the application of simple, sound leadership and management practices. Those skills were needed in the early Church, and they are needed in Christian camps today.*

---

## Conclusion

Sound, godly leadership and management practices saved the early Church's unity and allowed the Apostles to remain focused on their essential ministry of prayer and preaching. The dual dangers of division and distraction were thwarted through the application of simple, sound, universal leadership and management principles. Those skills were needed in the early Church, and they are needed in Christian camps today.

The success of any ministry is tied directly to God's grace and the application of God-given leadership and management principles and practices. The early Church used wise practices to survive these early hazards. In reality, these practices are not owned by the business community and then borrowed by ministries. They are God's universal truth, and applying God's truth benefits any organization, business, ministry, school, government, or camp.

The leaders of Christian camps today must avail themselves of the same practices that served the leaders of the early Church. This will ensure the long-term success of unified camp ministries that prayerfully connect their leaders to God and transform campers and guests through the effective teaching of God's Word.

The story ended well in Jerusalem. The miracle of the new Church continued. Even though we do not know the details, the passage concludes, *So the word of God spread. The number of disciples in Jerusalem increased rapidly, and a large number of priests became obedient to the faith* (v. 6:7). The revival continued, God's Word was preached, people responded, and even the religious leaders put their faith in Jesus Christ.

Ministry is complex; it was back then, and it is today. Innumerable, dangerous challenges beset us. Stay focused on prayer and biblical ministry. Stay unified in love. And utilize God's universal leadership and management practices that will keep camp running effectively.

*H*ere is a trustworthy saying: Whoever aspires to be an overseer desires a noble task.

*I Timothy 3:1*

### Chapter Eight
# Leadership Development
*I Timothy 3:1*

Christian camps produce leaders! Pastors, teachers, missionaries, youth directors, counselors, and a host of other ministry leaders cut their leadership and ministry teeth at Christian camps. But not just professional Christians – thousands of Sunday school teachers, youth workers, men's and women's ministry coordinators, and innumerable other volunteers started their ministry and leadership development at camp. Today's churches, schools, youth organizations, and service ministries are filled with people who discovered and developed their leadership and ministry gifts at camp.

---

*Today's churches, schools, youth organizations, and service ministries are filled with people who discovered and developed their leadership and ministry gifts at camp.*

---

Paul wrote a letter to his young friend and follower Timothy exhorting him to lead well despite his young age. He said, ***Don't let anyone look down on you because you*** *are young, but set an example for the believers in speech, in life, in love, in faith and in purity* (I Timothy 4:12). At an early age, Timothy shouldered significant responsibility; that is rare in many ministry contexts today. But camps are places where young people find opportunities to serve and lead early in life.

I was 14 years old when I started volunteering with a backpacking ministry, and I returned for several summers. My first job description was quite simple: gather the firewood, start the cooking fire, keep it going, make sure the cook had plenty of water, and of course anything else that needed to be done. During those teenage years, I led evening devotions (quite poorly at times), helped carry an injured camper several miles to the nearest road, searched for a runaway leader almost twice my age (a whole 'nother story), and scouted ahead to find safe places to set up camp. As a teenager, camp experiences provided me with tremendous opportunities to make mistakes yet surrounded me with wonderful people who helped me learn from my missteps and encouraged me to try again.

Paul taught young Timothy to stay focused on things that matter. *The goal of this command is love, which comes from a pure heart and a good conscience and a sincere faith* (I Timothy 1:5). Timothy needed a strong team of leaders to help him complete the many tasks that were required of him, and he also needed help to plan and lead wisely. But more than those, he needed accountability and role models to guide his personal expression of love, purity, and faith. His team was critical.

Before outlining the qualities of effective leaders, Paul made a brief, universal comment about leadership. He said, *Here is a trustworthy saying: If anyone sets his heart on being an overseer, he desires a noble task* (I Timothy 3:1). This verse is pregnant with *quadruplets*. Four fundamental leadership principles are packed within this short verse. They were important for young Timothy as he began his ministry, and they still ring true 2,000 years later.

## Aspiration

*First,* Paul addressed the issue of aspiration. He began, *If anyone sets his heart...* Is it okay to aspire to a position of leadership? YES! God designed each of us to lead. Genesis 1:26 describes the mysterious deliberation within the Godhead when human life was designed. *Then God said, Let us make man in our image, in our likeness, and let them rule over the fish of the sea and the birds of the air, over the livestock, over all the earth, and over all the creatures that move along the ground* (Genesis 1:26). Whatever else is involved in human design, the first thing mentioned is that people are to *rule over.* From the beginning God designed us to lead, but there is great variety in how we express that leadership.

The English word *aspires* is translated from the Greek word **oregetai** which carries the concept **to reach** or **to stretch**. This leadership challenge requires young leaders to stretch well beyond their comfort zone. Like the pole vaulter whose success is rewarded with a greater challenge and a higher goal, so too, effective young leaders are rewarded with increased responsibility.

Another picture could be of a first baseman stretching to receive a throw from shortstop. Uncomfortable, awkward, and a little off-balance but stretching as far as possible, reaching valiantly to fulfill his responsibilities. Stretching always takes us out of our comfort zone, but it is fundamental to leading well. We must aspire and stretch ourselves to meet the challenges leadership throws our way.

A dishwasher should aspire to become the assistant dish-room manager. The assistant dish-room manager should aspire to be the dish-room manager. The dish-room manager should aspire to be an assistant chef – and so on and so on. Aspiration is not bad in and of itself; we should examine our desires to insure that we are motivated by healthy means of fulfilling our needs.

---

 *A position of responsibility is just that – a role in which a person can succeed or fail.*

---

## Hold a Leadership Position

The verse's second focus is *positional leadership.* Paul next says, **If anyone sets his heart on being an overseer.** *Positional leadership* involves legitimate authority and flows from the office held or title associated with the job. *Personal leadership* is gained by mastering skills, gaining experience, and developing influence. Generally, *personal leadership* is touted as more valuable than *positional power.* Authority that flows from an individual's experience or mastery of a skill is seen as more significant than power that comes from holding a title or filling a position. The difference between *personal* and *positional* leadership styles can be seen when a highly skilled yet lower-ranked subordinate emerges as more capable than the inexperienced, ineffective, or incompetent person holding the leadership title. This difference comes into focus when the bullets begin to fly. Soldiers look to the battle-tested sergeant rather than the young lieutenant who is leading his first live-fire patrol. We should never underestimate the power and capability of the highly skilled sergeant over the newly commissioned lieutenant. However, *positional leadership* should not be undervalued. Accountability accompanies a position.

Positions of responsibility require leaders to get things done. Whether in a family or church, at work, or at camp, aspiration should be for much more than influence. Leaders should hold a responsible position and fulfill the mission assigned to that role. A position of responsibility is just that – a role in which a person can succeed or fail.

---

*Camps provide powerful settings for young people to test themselves and explore under utilized or unfamiliar gifts.*

---

When a leader accepts the responsibilities flowing from a title or office, he or she steps into the new, and at times, threatening arena of accountability. Either the job is done, or not. A new scorecard proclaims to the world whether the leader has found success or failure. *Personal leadership* is great, but *positional leaders* must perform.

Both are important. Personal leadership characteristics and qualities are essential, but positional leadership accepts responsibility and commits to fulfilling a mission. Leaders lead best when they develop personal skills and are willing to shoulder the responsibilities of a defined position. Camp provides a wonderful place for young staff members to develop their leadership gifts and to take on the responsibility of assigned tasks.

Some leaders have the capacity to do well; others struggle. Some leaders become stalled in their development. Camps provide powerful settings for young people to test themselves and explore under utilized or unfamiliar gifts. Lasagna pans are either clean or dirty. Chairs are set in an orderly manner or not. Lifeguards are on time, or the pool opens late. Within the reality of *responsibility* emerging leaders grow strong. Camps provide the positional responsibility for personal leadership to grow. These newly minted leaders often find root in other contexts outside of full-time camp ministry.

## Check Your Desires

Leaders are not always driven by pure motives. Unfortunately, self-centered desires are often the source of inappropriate leadership missteps. The *third* leadership issue Paul addresses is *desire*. On one hand, leadership deals with the social phenomena of how we relate to one another. Many suggest that the world can be divided between *leaders* and *followers* or by the slightly less onerous distinctions of *leaders* and *managers*. Whether leaders are born, developed, or both, the assumption is that we are either one or the other. That draws us to believe that we are either leaders or something else. And we know it is better to be a leader than to discover our nagging fears are actually true – we are a pathetic follower or lowly manager.

Psychological issues are probably even more controlling. We believe that leaders are powerful, wise, decisive, successful, rich, and have nice smiles. So, the more that we perceive ourselves as weak, unknowing, unsure, inept, and poor with crooked teeth, the more we desire a position of leadership to prop up our failing egos. In this case, the motivation to lead does not come from a desire to help others but from a need to help ourselves. Many hope that the mantle of leadership will provide an invisibility cloak to hide their shortcomings and insecurities.

---

 *Camp is a place where young staff members can develop their leadership abilities in an altruistic setting.*

---

Business, politics, and sadly some churches and camps have people in leadership positions who desire not to serve people but to be served by people – more and more people. And even more subtly, to be increasingly liked and admired.

The English word we translate *desire* has at its root the Greek word **epithumei**. The word literally means **to set your heart upon or to long for something**. It is used 16 times in the New Testament and about half of those times it expresses a negative attitude. Four times it is translated **lust** and three times **covet**. Camp is a place where young staff members can develop their leadership abilities in an altruistic setting. For the love of the Lord, the love of their co-workers, the love of the campers, and the love of the camp itself they will strive to lead well with God-honoring desires.

## Difficult Yet Noble Work

The final member of the leadership quadruplet is *work.* Leadership work is noble, but it is still work. Leadership is more than a line on a resume or a box to check on a college application. Leadership is not an honorary award for satisfactory service or length of employment. Leadership is hard and challenging work for several reasons, and this is especially true at camp.

*First,* volunteer ministry leaders must do their own work outside of camp as well. Church elders, members of a camp board, and volunteer counselors take time away from their families, sacrifice leisure activities, and still accomplish work obligations while investing in camp leadership. A volunteer camp leader must fulfill the many expected obligations of life but also find time to engage themselves in camp leadership activities. Sometimes they are pulled in too many directions and find it difficult to contribute all they would like.

*Second*, leaders must consider all perspectives. An attorney only needs to present his or her client's case as forcefully as possible, but a judge must weigh all sides fairly. Leaders must function as judges, listening wisely before courageously making informed godly decisions. But more than listening to various opinions and testing the direction of the wind, leaders must factor two additional issues into their decisions: *first*, they must discern what is ethically, morally, and biblically right. And *second,* they must determine what is strategically significant. At times, leaders must make unpopular decisions and do what is right ethically, morally, and biblically. At other times leaders must make unpopular decisions to accomplish the organizational goals and fulfil the mission.

*Third,* the challenge is multifaceted. The physical demands are substantial. Leadership is not easy; people allergic to hard work need not apply. Loads of laundry need to be washed, dried, and folded. Horses need to be fed, groomed, and saddled. Meals need to be prepared, served, and the dining area cleared and cleaned. Leaders must do their part, but they cannot do it alone and that means enlisting followers. Vince Lombardi, the great coach of the Green Bay Packers said, **Fatigue makes cowards of us all.**[6] And as the challenges move into the emotional, relational, and spiritual arenas, the nobility of the work becomes more problematic. When fatigue of body and soul overwhelm us, then, and only then, can **we mount up on wings of eagles** and lead with the strength that only God provides.

## Camp as a Leadership Incubator

Incubators provide a round-the-clock controlled environment in which eggs hatch and chicks quickly develop into independent, well-fed chickens. This temporary home is warm, safe, comfortable, and provides all the nourishment the chicks need to flourish and grow rapidly. But chickens don't live in the incubator; the goal is to grow rapidly, become strong, and leave the safe, controlled environment.

There are at least seven reasons Christian camps are excellent incubators to help young leaders grow rapidly.

---

*Eating meals, singing, playing, working, and at times crying together transfers the values and wisdom of one generation to the next.*

---

### Role Models

Leadership, like many things in life, is better caught than taught. Camp provides daily, life-on-life interactions between young staff and seasoned ministry veterans. We generally minister to those a few years behind us. In camp, high school volunteers learn from the college staff members, college staff members watch the young adults in leadership, and the young adults learn from the old pros. Eating meals, singing, playing, working, and at times crying together transfers the values and wisdom of one generation to the next.

### Close Supervision.

Camp is a place where little goes unnoticed. Positive peer pressure and strategic, caring leaders create a context to shape behavior. The high and persistent expectations at camp help modify young staff members' views of themselves, others, and God. The supervision is generally face-to-face. No e-mails or texts with long-distance observations and suggestions. Camp requires eyeball to eyeball interactions.

### Immediate Feedback.

At camp, there is no waiting until next Sunday to have the conversation, no lapsed time to come up with an excuse, and no gap in conversations to devise a rationalization. At camp issues are addressed in real time. Canoes left scattered on the shoreline and not placed on their racks is addressed today. Leaving the gate open to the pasture is confronted as soon as the horses are rounded up. Cabins late for breakfast, grass un-mowed, and archery equipment not locked are all teachable moments where young staff members either step up to greater responsibility or step out of the leadership pipeline.

### Supportive Community.

Camp people want everyone to succeed. They want to see growth and development in the lives of each camper and staff member. Very few gruff, angry, arrogant, or grumpy people are attracted to the Christian camping lifestyle. And if they do make it into a position of authority, they generally don't last long. Most leaders enter Christian camp ministry because they deeply desire to help others – campers and staff members. If anything, camp leaders tend to be overly accepting and shy away from confrontation. But the good ones, the ones who truly make a difference know how to organize, train, challenge, supervise, and evaluate their staff members, and reward the attitudes and behavior that makes camp great. Great camp leaders catch their staff members doing the right things and doing them well. They affirm tasks that are done properly and with godly attitudes. They model support and affirmation, and they expect that leadership style to be replicated at every level of their team.

---

*The immensity and intensity of the work creates pressure that strengthens young leadership muscles.*

---

### Hard Work.

Camp work is exhausting. Someone has said, **the hardest job you will ever love is serving as a counselor at a Christian camp**. The hours are long, and the responsibility is relentless. **Where is Amos? Did Maria take her medicine? Kendrick, this is the fourth day you have worn that shirt! Cat, can I comb your hair?** It's like becoming an instant parent of eight 10-year-olds, and learning to teach archery, soccer, and arts and crafts as well as lead Bible study and devotions, and have meaningful conversations with each camper. And that is just the counselors. Someone gets to dig through 30 bags of kitchen garbage to find the retainer Larry left on his lunch tray. The horses need grooming, the toilet is clogged in Bluebonnet Lodge, the tractor will not start, 26 pans of semi-burned lasagna need to be scraped and washed, and the swimming pool is cloudy again today! The *immensity* and *intensity* of the work creates pressure that strengthens young leadership muscles. All gain strength, but some staff members seem to bulk up more than others. For many men and women, camp is the place where leadership skills emerge that will serve them well for a lifetime.

---

 *Camp staff members are rewarded for faithful service with greater challenges and opportunities for more faithful service in the days ahead.*

---

### Incremental Advancement.

Camp provides opportunities for young people to face greater challenges every summer, if not every week! A young girl serving as a counselor-in-training can return the following summer as a counselor, the next year as a senior counselor, and by year four, she may migrate into a program director role. Wherever she winds up, she will continue to use the leadership skills that develop every step of the way. The leadership stretching becomes more intense with each advancement. Camp staff members are rewarded for faithful service with greater challenges and opportunities for more faithful service in the days ahead. Many times, these growth steps continue in camp but often, the skills acquired are applied in other areas of life and ministry.

### The Spirit of God.

Amazing transformation happens at camp, but God is not confined to work only at Christian camps. The goal is never to create a following or establish our institutions; the goal is always to **make disciples**. And the Spirit of God empowers and superintends every aspect of that disciple making process. Camp utilizes an amazing context where time away in a new setting, immersion into creation, deepening relationships, and spiritual focus come together and are bathed in prayer. God uses camps to draw many people into a new relationship with Him through faith in Jesus Christ. Many more are trained, inspired, and encouraged in their walk with God. And some, often the staff members, develop ministry and leadership skills that they will employ the rest of their lives.

## *Conclusion*

Christian camps provide the controlled environment for rapid leadership development. They are places where God works powerfully and continually to round off the rough edges of our lives, transforming us into more useful servants. When our daughters were young, my wife and I acquired a lapidary machine, a small contraption with a cylinder attached to a motor that tumbled rocks over and over night and day until they became smooth, polished stones. The process was simple: we filled the tube with water, sand, and a few rough rocks, then we sat the machine on our front porch and turned on the motor. For more than two weeks the tube incessantly rotated, continuously tumbling the contents. The process was laborious and relentless but once opened, the stones emerged with most of the rough edges worn off. The lapidary machine did in a few weeks what the natural setting may have never accomplished. So too, camps accelerate the leadership development process, smoothing rough edges and changing the participants forever.

Leadership is worthy of our aspiration, and camp will stretch and grow leaders in significant ways. Taking on a position of leadership means greater responsibility and accountability. The role can be risky, painful, and challenging. Some people desire leadership roles with ignoble hearts. Leaders must always ask themselves the hard questions concerning motivation. They must be willing to look deep inside to determine whether their leadership desire is to fulfill an unmet personal need or to use their gifts for the good of the community. And leadership is hard work – noble work, but hard work.

Camp is a great place for young leaders to emerge. Role models, close supervision, immediate feedback, supportive community, hard work, incremental advancement opportunities, and the Spirit of God come together to accelerate the development of young leaders. The continual tumbling and consistent pressure smooth the rough edges and polish many young people, preparing them for the next challenge God has in store.

*Camps accelerate the leadership development process, smoothing rough edges and changing the participants forever.*

The Lord appeared to Abraham near the great trees of Mamre while he was sitting at the entrance to his tent in the heat of the day. ²Abraham looked up and saw three men standing nearby. When he saw them, he hurried from the entrance of his tent to meet them and bowed low to the ground.

³He said, "If I have found favor in your eyes, my lord, do not pass your servant by. ⁴Let a little water be brought, and then you may all wash your feet and rest under this tree. ⁵Let me get you something to eat, so you can be refreshed and then go on your way—now that you have come to your servant."

"Very well," they answered, "do as you say."

⁶So Abraham hurried into the tent to Sarah. "Quick," he said, "get three seahs of the finest flour and knead it and bake some bread."

⁷Then he ran to the herd and selected a choice, tender calf and gave it to a servant, who hurried to prepare it.

⁸He then brought some curds and milk and the calf that had been prepared, and set these before them. While they ate, he stood near them under a tree.

*Genesis 18:1-8*

## Chapter Nine
# A Ministry of Hospitality[7]
*Genesis 18:1-8*

The Apostle Paul lists the ideal qualities for a local church leader in 1 Timothy 3:2 and Titus 1:8. Both of these lists include *hospitality*. When vetting the next generation of church leaders, the focus tends to be on family issues, emotional stability, alcohol consumption, and biblical commitment, but we generally give prospective leaders a pass on hospitality. Admittedly, hospitality was culturally more significant in biblical days. Twenty-first century western culture has drifted into self-centered independence, allowing us to blow past hospitality as a non-issue. But for the early Church, hospitality was a big deal, and it should be important to us as well.

---

*Hospitality reminds us that even though campers may be strangers, they must be loved.*

---

Surprise, surprise, Christian camping is all about hospitality! Hospitality, *philoxenia* in Greek, literally means *the love* (philos) *of strangers* (xenos). Every week, thousands of campers show up at sites throughout this country and around the world. People with hurts and needs, questions and worries, joys and opportunities. Camp staff members may know campers' names and hometowns, they may have a brief report on their background, or they may remember their face from a previous summer or weekend retreat, but most campers arrive bringing brand new or very warmed-over relationships. Hospitality reminds us that even though campers may be strangers, they must be loved.

The camp setting and program are generally designed to stimulate relational development. Within the first moments of arrival at camp, the *philoxenia* should be evident. Camp staff members serve as the great *lovers of strangers*, and camp is a place where the next generation of Christian leaders can develop lifestyles committed to hospitality.

Genesis 18:1-7 provides an amazing model of hospitality. Even though the events occurred thousands of years ago in a very different cultural context, the hospitality principles in this story provide a framework for every camp, center, retreat, or outdoor adventure today.

## The Story

Abraham was a shepherd, a nomad, a wanderer. He, along with his family and entourage of servants and workers, lived in tents. They worked hard, but they also worked smart and when the sun got hot, they took a break. Our story begins, **The LORD appeared to Abraham near the great trees of Mamre while he was sitting at the entrance to his tent in the heat of the day** (Genesis 18:1). The heat of the day was rest time. The hot sun of the Middle East called for a break, and Abraham obliged.

---

*Abraham took the responsibility to make these strangers feel welcome, and he initiated the conversation.*

---

The plot thickens.

*Abraham looked up and saw three men standing nearby. When he saw them, he hurried from the entrance of his tent to meet them and bowed low to the ground. He said, "If I have found favor in your eyes, my lord, do not pass your servant by. Let a little water be brought, and then you may all wash your feet and rest under this tree. Let me get you something to eat, so you can be refreshed and then go on your way--now that you have come to your servant." (v. 2-5a)*

At an inconvenient time, when Abraham was hot, tired, and had other expectations for his afternoon, a need presented itself and Abraham responded. His engagement with these strangers demonstrates eight important principles of hospitality.

## Take Initiative

Abraham initiated the conversation. In his culture, guests may have waited nearby in a conspicuous manner, hoping to be invited into a compound of tents for provision and security, but it was up to the host to extend the invitation. Hospitality depends upon the host's initiation. *Hello. Please come in. Hi, my name is...... Won't you join us?* And so on. Abraham took the lead, welcoming the strangers into his world. He had the upper hand – the power was all his. He controlled the compound, he owned the food and water, and he could extend or reserve his care. Abraham took the responsibility to make these strangers feel welcome, and he initiated the conversation.

## Honor Guests

*Abraham honored his guests.* He bowed to the ground and showed them respect. He didn't begin by sizing them up to see whether they were worthy of his care and concern; he just humbled himself and took on the role of a servant. He provided a genuine offer to help before he knew their status or standing in life. Even though he held a position of power, Abraham humbled himself and assumed the posture of a servant, ready to assist these strangers. This had to make his guests feel good. And making people feel special is a key to true hospitality.

## Offer Assistance

Abraham was not pushy. He simply made himself available and offered assistance along with some specific suggestions. The Hebrew construction is a linguistic form not found in English. It is halfway between a command and a simple statement. *If I have found favor... Let a little water be brought... Let me get you something to eat...*

---

*Hospitality requires immediate attention and a willingness to meet real needs in real time.*

---

Never demanding, but also insistent. Not domineering but offering specific options: *stay here a while, let me provide refreshment, and let me feed you.* Hospitality is not controlling; it offers assistance and seeks the best interest of the guest. True hospitality should never be offered to fulfill an unhealthy need or desire by the host or hostess to be liked or appreciated. Genuine hospitality is a legitimate offer to help. Hospitality for Abraham flowed from a genuine interest in the well-being of his guests. His motive was evidenced by providing for their physical comfort – food, water, shade – but it also assumed their total care and protection. Abraham was not trying to impress his neighbors or be highly esteemed on social media. He just knew it was the right thing to do – and he did it.

The story continues.

> *So Abraham hurried into the tent to Sarah. "Quick," he said, "get three seahs of fine flour and knead it and bake some bread." Then he ran to the herd and selected a choice, tender calf and gave it to a servant, who hurried to prepare it. (v. 6-7)*

---

*Way too often we try to tackle projects all by ourselves, trying our best to appear capable, strong, and efficient.*

---

## Serve Quickly

The story picks up the pace considerably from a lazy afternoon siesta to a frantic mobilization to serve the strangers. Abraham **hurried**. He told Sarah and the others to do their work **quickly**. He **ran** to the herd to select the calf. Then the servants **hurried** to prepare the meal. This was an intense, focused, coordinated effort to meet the needs of the strangers in a short time frame. When people are hungry, they need food. When they are tired, they need rest. When they are lonely, they need a friend. Hospitality requires immediate attention and a willingness to meet real needs in real time. Lazy, lackluster hospitality is never appropriate. Nonchalant hospitality sends an inconsistent message and creates counterproductive outcomes. A slow response says other things are more important than you. Whereas a prompt response says you are the most important issue in my life, at least right now.

## Engage Others

Abraham didn't try to meet all the needs by himself; he *engaged others* and delegated the work. First, he involved Sarah then he engaged his servants. While speaking to some Christian camping leaders in Kenya, I asked the familiar question, **How do you eat an elephant**? I expected the standard response, **One bite at a time,** but I received blank stares. A young Kenyan stopped me after the seminar and asked, **Why would anyone try to eat an elephant by himself? If you have an elephant to eat, call the whole village!** My American bias (and ignorance) was showing. Way too often we try to tackle projects all by ourselves, trying our best to appear capable, strong, and efficient. But generally, true hospitality requires a team effort. We need family and friends to join us to meet the needs of others. We have limited skills, gifts, time, and energy. We need others to contribute to meet the needs of strangers.

## Give Your Best

Abraham's unexpected guests did not provide an opportunity for him to clean out the leftovers in the refrigerator or use up the last crumbs in the potato chip bag. He gave his best. Abraham personally selected a choice calf, probably one that was being prepared for a special occasion. Not bad food, not ok food; instead, he offered his guests the best food available. Abraham demonstrated serious hospitality in the food service arena, and camps should too. The old camp adage is true, **They will forgive you for bad theology, but never for bad food.** But giving our best should extend beyond the kitchen. Our guests need the best programs, the best staff, the best Bible studies, the best singing, the best registration process, and the best of everything else. Hospitality provides our guests with the best of whatever we have.

## Give Abundantly

Abraham **gave abundantly.** A whole calf for three people? Sarah prepared about 20 quarts of flour, that's a lot of bread for three people, even if they were famished from their journey. Family and servants probably also partook of the ample supply of food. True hospitality gives generously, above and beyond expectations. Hospitality does not require reckless spending or irresponsible behavior, but it does call us to avoid scrimping on the basics or being stingy with what we have. Loving strangers means creating a context where guests feel less intrusive and genuinely welcomed. We do not want to be wasteful, but at the same time we want our guests to experience a sense of freedom and abundance. The more we meet physical needs, the more we will create a context of trust and security. Upon that safe and satisfied foundation of fulfilled physical needs, camp staff members can build emotional, relational, and spiritual trust as well.

---

*Upon that safe and satisfied foundation of fulfilled physical needs, camp staff members can build emotional, relational, and spiritual trust as well.*

---

## Do Not Intrude

Abraham gave his guests space and did not intrude unnecessarily into their lives. He engaged them and remained available, but he allowed them to have room to relax. This permitted his guests to remain unencumbered by expectations they may have felt or obligations that might have projected into the situation—they could just relax! **While** *they ate, he stood near them under a tree* (v.18:8b). He remained close; they did not have to hunt to find him if a problem occurred. He strategically situated himself nearby but outside of their company and conversation. Too often, camping leaders violate boundaries and intrude into guest groups' space. There are rules that must be followed and safety concerns that must be expressed, but in general, camping leaders should strive to find the balance between abandoning guest groups to their own devices and hovering over their every move. Abraham seemed to find the sweet spot, standing under a nearby tree. Available, but not in the way. Ready to serve, but not intruding unnecessarily into the lives of his guests.

## Conclusion

Abraham's guests turned out to be angels on a special mission from God, and they proclaimed a huge blessing to Sarah and Abraham – their promised son. There is no telling who the campers you show hospitality to may become or what blessing they may bring to you and others.

Christian camping is all about loving strangers. Father Abraham provided a model for us to follow and set a high standard for us to pursue. The principles he applied and demonstrated thousands of years ago still work today. Treating people well and loving strangers never goes out of style.

*The end of all things is near. Therefore be alert and of sober mind so that you may pray. ⁸ Above all, love each other deeply, because love covers over a multitude of sins. ⁹ Offer hospitality to one another without grumbling. ¹⁰ Each of you should use whatever gift you have received to serve others, as faithful stewards of God's grace in its various forms. ¹¹ If anyone speaks, they should do so as one who speaks the very words of God. If anyone serves, they should do so with the strength God provides, so that in all things God may be praised through Jesus Christ. To him be the glory and the power for ever and ever. Amen.*

*I Peter 4:7-11*

## Chapter Ten

# Program Versus Operations
*I Peter 4:7-11*

Peter's first letter was addressed to frightened Christians scattered throughout what is now Turkey. Threatened and persecuted, they ran for their lives. When Peter writes, **The end of all things is at hand** (I Peter 4:7), he is not using colorful, figurative language; he is powerfully and directly addressing their clear and present danger. The original recipients of Peter's letter read these words with much more intensity than most of us today who are living in comfortable and secure settings. These words – **The end of all things is at hand** – capture the setting into which Peter writes his powerful instruction, explaining the attitudes and behaviors these refugees needed to finish well. Peter was no stranger to life and death moments. He had experienced a few real-life events that probably came flashing back as he

---

*When time becomes short, we discover our true priorities. Deadlines reveal what is truly important to us; small stuff is set aside, and mission critical tasks become our sole focus.*

---

penned these words. He might have remembered a storm on the Sea of Galilee pounding their boat and threatening to drown him and the other disciples while Jesus slept. And the time he walked on water toward Jesus only to feel the cold waves creep up his ankles and legs. Certainly, the Garden of Gethsemane was on his mind, where he pulled a sword and single-handedly attacked the angry mob threatening to arrest Jesus. Later, imprisoned in Jerusalem, Peter fully expected to face execution like his dear friend James. Yes, he looked death in the eye numerous times and came out stronger, wiser, and better equipped to help others.

Concerned for those Christians running from persecution and with vivid memories of his own life-threatening experiences etched in his mind, Peter wrote, **the end of all things is at hand.**

## The First Hinge – Therefore

Peter next introduces the first of two critical hinge words in this passage, *therefore*. **Therefore** looks back to an established fact and looks forward to a desired action. **Therefore** builds the rational basis for the next steps forward. The critically important point that Peter wants to make is, *time is running out!*

When time becomes short, we discover our true priorities. Deadlines reveal what is most important to us; small stuff is set aside, and mission critical tasks become our sole focus. Intensity increases. Energy and adrenaline are released to accomplish what really matters. Resources are redirected to the areas of greatest need. *The end of all things changes our perspective on everything.*

Peter outlines a seven-step plan for anyone staring into the end of all things. All seven are crucial; they provide us guidance for living life with godly priorities and clear intentions. The final two steps, however, speak directly to the Christian camping context.

## *Think Clearly*

First and foremost, Peter says a clear mind is fundamental. *Thinking clearly* (v. 7) is essential if we are to respond well in a crisis. Max DePree said, *The first responsibility of leadership is to define reality.*[8] Clear thinking is critical if we are to perceive reality. Like Elisha's servant, we see the enemy surrounding us and miss the chariots of fire surrounding them (2 Kings 6:8-23).

The word translated *thinking clearly*, **sophronesate**, is used only one other time in the New Testament, and that story provides a powerful picture into its meaning. Jesus encounters a wild man possessed by a legion of demons. He has been abusing himself and harassing the local population. Jesus liberates the man from the hoard of demons, and they invade a herd of pigs. This wild-eyed, crazy man, who ran naked in a cemetery, cut himself, ripped off chains, and terrorized the locals, was radically transformed by his encounter with Jesus. Luke describes three major changes in the man's behavior. They found the man from whom the demons had gone out, sitting at Jesus' feet, dressed, and in his right mind. (Luke 8:35). *First*, he was sitting at Jesus' feet, in submission to his Lord and learning all he could. *Second*, he was wearing clothes, respecting himself and others and conforming to the decency standards of society. And *third*, he was in his *right mind*. The word describing his mental, emotional, and spiritual improvement is from the same root as Peter's choice in I Peter 4:7. The fog that confused and confounded him lifted, and after his encounter with Jesus, he clearly saw the reality of life. And so should we.

## Self-Control

After thinking clearly, we need to respond to life's challenges with self-control (v. 7). Thinking correctly and acting responsibly go hand-in-hand, and both are critical in the face of a serious threat. Peter clearly saw the threat of the mob that came to arrest Jesus. He understood the threat, but his behavior was an uncontrolled reaction; he grabbed a sword and sliced off an ear. Peter was known for speaking impulsively and acting rashly. His life as a disciple was marked by impetuous behavior. But he wrote this book at least 25 years after Jesus' death and resurrection. For 25 years, the Holy Spirit had been producing fruit in his life, and one of those fruits is self-control. Responding, not reacting, requires clear mindedness coupled with self-control.

Self-control has two parts: the assertive, *yes, I will* part and the stubborn, *no, I won't* part. In Colossians, Paul prays that the Christians in Colossae (whom he had never met) might **be strengthened with all power according to his glorious might so that you may have great endurance and patience** (Colossians 1:11). The strength Paul prayed for them was to be demonstrated in both *endurance* and *patience*. They needed *endurance* to keep going and the *patience* to wait. A friend of mine says, I've never met an exercise plan I can't out eat. We need the strength of self-control to do two things, faithfully exercise and stay on our diet! Self-control says *yes* and *no*.

## Pray

The often overlooked yet most reasonable and responsible response to a crisis is prayer. It is the response that flows from thinking clearly and being under control. God is the provider of everything that we need: wisdom, strength, courage, direction, endurance, peace, and more. Like any loving and wise Father, He is eager to give us what we truly need and provide what is in our best interest. We just need to ask. He is strong enough, wise enough, and loving enough to hear the outpourings of our hearts. He will provide direction if we ask and wait for His reply.

Peter knew a little bit about prayer and Jesus' ability to respond. When he began to sink, ending his walk with Jesus upon the waves of the Sea of Galilee, he prayed a simple, authentic, yet powerful prayer of request: **Lord, save me** (Matthew 14:30). And Jesus did.

When their ship was being tossed in the storm and this seasoned fisherman feared for his life, Peter simply vented his frustration to Jesus who was asleep in the back of the boat, **Teacher, don't you care if we drown?** (Mark 4:38). And Jesus stilled the storm.

But in the Garden, as the mob arrived intending to arrest Jesus, unnamed disciples ask Jesus for direction. But Peter responded without waiting for the reply. When Jesus' followers saw what was going to happen, they said, **Lord, should we strike with our sword**? And one of them struck the servant of the high priest, cutting off his right ear. Only Doctor Luke records the amazing conclusion. But Jesus answered, **'No more of this!' And he touched the man's ear and healed him** (Luke 22:49-50). Over the years, Peter had learned to talk to God, and he directed his readers to talk to God and trust Him in the good times and the bad.

## Love

After we look to God in *prayer*, we are to look to others in *love*. Our natural response to a crisis is selfishness. Self-preservation dominates our motives and actions. Unless we intentionally commit to loving others and focus on meeting the needs of those around us, we will become self-absorbed and consumed with our own needs. Peter went on to say, *love covers a multitude of sins* (1 Peter 4:8). There are two sides to love's covering work—*preventive* and *responsive.* Love restrains us from committing sins against the people around us. However, when others commit sins against us, love allows us to treat those misdeeds with intentional disregard. It may be impossible to forget, but we can forgive and let go of toxic bitterness and destructive grudges.

## Hospitality

The natural outpouring of love demonstrates hospitality to those we encounter. *(Chapter 9 deals with hospitality in detail.)* Hospitality validates the love we espouse. Literally, hospitality (philoxenia) means, **the love of strangers.** Loving strangers is what happens at Christian camp. Strangers arrive every week during summer camp, and they are loved.

Hospitality becomes authentic when it is done with the right attitude. Peter may have been sitting in the back of a few summer-staff meetings; he added the warning, **without complaining** (v. 9). Some of the campers who annoy us the most are the ones in greatest need of God's love.

My first summer as a camp counselor the staff met for a brief prayer time after every breakfast. One morning I listened as an older counselor shared about his challenging campers. He said, *I prayed all night long, but when the sun came up, they were still there!* The goal of hospitality is not to eliminate problems but to love strangers with a pure heart and serve them with the love of Christ.

## Speak and Serve

The final two statements are really one directive. We are to serve one another, and Peter explains two ways that may occur. Peter says, *Each one should use whatever gift he has received to serve others, faithfully administering God's grace in its various forms* (v. 10). Serving one another is an individualized assignment. We are to use whatever gift we have received to help others. But engagement generally falls into one of two broad areas: *speaking* or *acts of physical service.*

Peter begins by identifying the first way to serve—*verbally. If anyone speaks, he should do it as one speaking the very words of God* (v. 11). He then focuses on the second and equally important opportunity to serve—*physically. If anyone serves, he should do it with the strength God provides* (v. 11).

Camps depend upon people utilizing both *speaking* gifts and *serving* gifts.[9] Counselors, musicians, speakers, program directors, and recreation leaders are the voice of the camp. They share the message in word, song, and relationships. But just as necessary are the people working in food service, registration, maintenance, housekeeping, and those cleaning up after the horses.

Camp can become divided between program (speaking) and operations (physical serving). The program staff tends to be spontaneous, fun, high-profile, and they sometimes color outside the lines. The operations staff tend to be systems thinkers, work sequentially, and follow orderly patterns. Bottom line, program staff members often make the messes that the operations staff members must clean up. And operations staff often set rules that the program staff have to follow.

---

*We all need to play our unique part expressing our giftedness to the best of our ability. One gift is not better, more necessary, or more significant than any other.*

---

While on summer staff at a family camp, some of us would stay up late volunteering to taste test leftover desserts. Eventually the conversation would migrate to the events of the day, and we would review the antics of the children. A name would come up and after a story or two of disobedience, creativity, misadventure, or some attention-gaining stunt, someone would predict the camper's future role on summer staff, **Program. *Definitely program***. And the rest, like a jury that had reached a verdict, would affirm, **Program**. Another round of stories would focus on a child who worked all day in crafts making an intricately designed Bible cover, offered to help in the dish room, or spent free time watching the maintenance staff repairing a fence. **Operations**, chimed a knowledgeable voice, and several others in the room voiced their agreement. People have different abilities and unique personalities, and many express them early in life. But everyone has a role to play and a gift to contribute to an effective ministry.

We tend to think that we are a sheep or a goat – one or the other, program or operations. And truly, some people have speaking gifts and others have serving gifts. But life is generally not that clear cut. We all need to be able to speak and serve as the need arises. At times we all wash dishes. And everyone needs to be able to share the Gospel when an opportunity presents itself. We all need to play our unique part expressing our giftedness to the best of our ability. One gift is not better, more necessary, or more significant than any other. All successful camps require strong performances by those in *speaking* roles and those in *physical serving* roles.


## The Second Hinge – So That

We now encounter the second powerful hinge in these verses, *so that*. Peter says, *so that in all things God may be praised through Jesus Christ. To him be the glory and the power for ever and ever. Amen* (v. 11).

*So that* looks ahead and focuses our attention on the desired results. All these activities – thinking clearly, self-control, prayer, love, hospitality, speaking, and physically serving – establish the platform for the *so that*. The purpose of all this behavior is to bring praise and glory to God. Our story is never *THE* story. Our story is always a *subplot* in God's grand drama. This is not to say that our story is insignificant; quite the contrary, our story plays an important part in the big story. It is just not *THE* story. The story is always about Jesus, not about us.

## Conclusion

When **the end of all things is at hand**, the truly important issues become clear: thinking clearly, acting with control, praying, expressing love, speaking the truth of God, and serving others.

We never know what day will be our last, so we should make it our priority to be about the things that Peter describes as central to a healthy, focused life. But we must also remember that each camp, conference, retreat, or adventure has an ending. The final day, final night, final morning of camp are critical moments and should be planned intentionally and executed with great precision.

Are campers and staff thinking clearly? Are they making wise decisions?

Are people responding to the end of camp with self-controlled, intentional, strategic actions?

Is there time set aside for prayer, commitment, and connection with God?

Are opportunities available for healthy, godly expressions of love to one another?

Is hospitality demonstrated to the very end?

Are campers given the challenge that someday they might return as staff members, whether speaking or serving?

Most of all, is camp ending with a focus on the glory of God? Is He the one who is praised and honored for the successes and victories of the week?

*The end of all things is at hand, therefore ...*

*Therefore everyone who hears these words of mine and puts them into practice is like a wise man who built his house on the rock. 25 The rain came down, the streams rose, and the winds blew and beat against that house; yet it did not fall, because it had its foundation on the rock. 26 But everyone who hears these words of mine and does not put them into practice is like a foolish man who built his house on sand. 27 The rain came down, the streams rose, and the winds blew and beat against that house, and it fell with a great crash."*

*Matthew 7:24-27*

## Chapter Eleven
# Follow-Up
*Matthew 7:24-27*

Many years ago, I delivered a parcel of brochures to one of our supporting churches. I handed them to the receptionist and visited briefly with one of the associate pastors then headed out the door.

As I walked down the long sidewalk toward the camp van, my departure was interrupted by a woman's voice. I turned and saw a lady hurrying from the church toward me. She had been in the office when I handed off the literature. She smiled and asked if I was with the camp. I replied that I was and wondered what was coming next. The story she told I will never forget.

She relayed how some neighborhood children had invited her son to attend our camp during a previous summer. As concerned parents, they had some misgivings because of the camp's Christian orientation. They were not believers, but neither were they antagonistic toward Christianity or any religion – just skeptical and not at all interested. After a short discussion they decided to let their son attend; *what could it hurt if he got a little religion?* So, they signed him up.

He had a great time at camp and while there, he trusted Christ as his Savior. When he returned home, dominoes began to fall – he wanted to go to church. Mom and sister played along; they ended up attending the neighborhood church where we were now standing. There they, too, heard the good news and trusted Christ. A few months later Dad had also become a follower of Jesus. Within a few months of summer camp, their entire family's destiny was altered, and life would never be the same.

With tears in her eyes, she thanked me for the impact the camp had made on her son and her family. I assured her that God was the one who changes lives – the camp was just the tool God used to do His work in the life of their son and family.

That encounter reminded me that only eternity will tell the hidden results of a week of camp. God is at work way beyond the fences of our acreage and way past the closing day's teary-eyed goodbyes. Now, fifty years since my teenage summers on staff at camp, I have seen the ripple effect extend for generations.

The story surfaces the ongoing question – what about the impact of camp once the week or weekend is over? Sometimes the sparks of camp ignite a bonfire back home, and sometimes the flame appears to be snuffed out. How can camps influence campers the rest of the year – or the rest of their lives? And possibly more puzzling is the question, *should they?*

Jesus's longest sermon, the Sermon on the Mount (Matthew 5-7), is filled with rich pictures, challenging exhortation, and some deeply needed how-to-do-its. In His closing illustration, Jesus painted a vivid picture of two men, two foundations, two houses, and one storm. In Jesus' story, both men are builders; they both construct houses. The houses look very similar; the only difference is the foundation. One is built on a rock, the other on sand. And then the storm blew in. The rain came down. The water rose. The wind beat against the houses. The one on the rock withstood the storm, and the one on the sand was destroyed.

---

*One of camp's strengths is that it combines the theoretical and the practical – the classroom and the laboratory.*

---

So, what does the foundation represent? What made the difference in the two houses? What provided strength and security? What led to ruin?  Fortunately, we do not have to speculate; the Bible is very clear. Jesus began His illustration with the simple declaration, ***everyone who hears these words of Mine and puts then into practice is like a wise man*** (Matthew 7:24a). And equally clear is the follow-up statement, ***everyone who hears these words of***

*Mine and does not put them into practice is like a foolish man* (Matthew 7:26a). Jesus' point is that applying God's truth to our lives is what gives us the strength and stability to withstand the storms of life. Likewise, failing to put into practice the truth God provides leaves us vulnerable to the wind and flood water that will surely come our way.

---

*Camps are not built for long-term follow-up. They offer one-off events and provide significant short-term influences in peoples' spiritual development. But camps are supplemental events not designed for ongoing input, care, encouragement, and accountability.*

---

One of camp's strengths is that it combines the theoretical and the practical – the classroom and the laboratory. Not only does camp provide a compressed time for intense biblical instruction, it also offers opportunity to practice the lessons learned in real time. How do we respond to conflict and disappointment? Camp provides us a chance to apply what we have learned through those tough moments! How do we show love to the unlovely? Camp provides a great place to practice gracious behavior. How do we forgive our enemies? Situations might arise during the week of camp where we must deal with conflict. The skin-on-skin interactions of a camp experience provide plenty of opportunities to practice what we have heard preached. Camp creates a safe, integrated, and supportive context for compressed learning and immediate application.

The strength and stability of our Christian life hinges to some degree on what we know. Biblical and theological learning is very important. However, to a much greater degree, our spiritual development is based upon our willingness to apply what we have learned. What we do with what we know is crucial. Our stability in the face of storms is based upon our response to God's truth before the gale-force winds begin to blow.

Campers learn that the truth of God's Word works at camp, but will it work back at home? How do camps encourage and help campers continue applying what they learned once they return to the routines of home and the influence of friends?

---

*Camps, by definition, are temporary communities. They provide a short-term spiritual banquet, not long-term spiritual nourishment.*

---

Many see the Achilles' heel of camp ministry as follow-up. That concern is legitimate in some ways, yet very misleading. Camps are not built for long-term follow-up. They offer one-off events and provide significant short-term influences in peoples' spiritual development. But camps are supplemental events not designed for ongoing input, care, encouragement, and accountability.

Let's unpack the camp follow-up dilemma in six ways.

## Great Idea

*First,* let's remember that follow-up is a good thing! Continuing contact, providing training materials, developing year-round Bible clubs, online instruction, or after-camp devotional studies are all great! Ongoing spiritual input is critical, but camps are not designed for long-term influence. Their specialty is *event impact.* Ongoing spiritual influence is essential, but most camps do not have the staff or resources to engage this challenge well or for the long-term. To the extent that it is possible, staying engaged with campers is a worthwhile endeavor, but not always practical. Camps need to find the best possible avenues to encourage their campers in a lifetime of spiritual growth, and that will generally mean partnering with churches or other local ministries.

---

 *During one week of camp, hearts are opened, sins confessed, commitments made, and new directions set.*

---

## No Guilt

*Second,* let's not feel guilty for camps not doing what they were not designed to do! Camps, by definition, are *temporary* communities. They provide a short-term spiritual banquet, not long-term spiritual nourishment. That is not a bad thing. People need feasts occasionally, but they also need regular, well-balanced spiritual meals.

Changing the imagery, camp ministries provide a series of spiritual booster shots to help start, secure, stimulate, and strengthen campers in their Christian lives. Year after year, event after event, God is working to generate a cumulative impact in campers' lives. The result of those sequential events can be much more significant than what any singular event could achieve.

Short-term, temporary communities are what camp provides. But just because camp is not designed for long-term influence does not mean that a camper's spiritual development is not significant – quite the contrary. Camps need to unapologetically do what camps do. But they also need to cooperate with and encourage institutions that provide spiritual sustenance day after day, week after week, and year after year. As critical as camps are, they are only part of God's big design.

## *Local Church*

*Third*, let's remember that involvement in a healthy, local church is fundamental for long-term spiritual growth. I often feel sorry for church staff, Sunday school teachers, and volunteers who work faithfully 51 weeks a year and sometimes see little outward change in the children and young people in their ministry. During one week of camp, hearts are opened, sins confessed, commitments made, and new directions set. The life-changing events of camp flow from the faithful prayer, strategic preparation, and tenacious service during the preceding year. That consistent biblical input is critical before camp and essential after campers return home.

The church, in turn, benefits from the new and deeper commitments made at camp. Ministry is a cooperative privilege. As Paul reminded the Corinthians, ***I planted the seed, Apollos watered it, but God made it grow. So, neither he who plants nor he who waters is anything, but only God, who makes things grow. The man who plants and the man who waters have one purpose, and each will be rewarded according to his own labor*** (1 Corinthians 3:6-8). As much as possible, churches and camps must intertwine their efforts, remembering that ***neither he who plants nor he who waters is anything but only God, who makes things grow.***

## Family and Church

*Fourth,* let's remember that God has established the Church and the family to nurture the next generation. Depending on the context and purpose, some camps focus on supporting families in their efforts to develop faith in the lives of children, youth, and in some cases adults. Other camps direct their efforts toward helping local churches fulfill their missions. Neither is right, neither is wrong, but both should be strategic and support families and local churches as best they can. These two God-ordained institutions, church and the family, meet camper needs the other 51 weeks a year; therefore, camps maximize their impact as they cooperate with families and local churches. The wonderful things learned and practiced at camp come into full bloom when they are applied within the family structure and the ministry of the local church.

## Be Responsible

*Fifth,* let's be responsible. Many camps target unreached and unchurched young people with a desire to see them come to faith in Christ. These evangelistically oriented camps attract many campers from homes with little spiritual commitment and without local church roots. They need camp, they need the good news of God's love, grace, and forgiveness, and they need a church home! Camp ministries that target these campers carry the greatest burden for direct, ongoing follow-up. Even though camp is designed to be a short-term experience, the campers' ongoing spiritual development is critically important. Camps that focus on unbelieving campers must shoulder the responsibility of helping them continue to grow spiritually and eventually integrate into a healthy, local church.

## God is Sovereign

*Sixth,* let's remember that God is in control. I had no idea what God was doing through the life of the young camper whose one-week experience at camp rippled through his entire family. God was working way beyond my awareness to accomplish supernatural transformation in the life of a family that needed help. God's sovereign super-intending of events does not relieve us of our responsibility to work strategically and effectively to serve our campers and guests as well as we can. But it does remind us that *He* is in control, and we are along for the ride. We must work hard and responsibly, but we must always hold our plans in open hands and ask Him to blow away the chaff of any of our strategies that do not coincide with His.

## Conclusion

Camp plays a unique and important role in the spiritual development of millions of campers each year. But camp is only one, short-term yet significant part of the picture.

Cooperation and coordination within the body of Christ is essential. There is no room for turf warfare within God's army.

Applying what we know of God's Word provides strength and stability in all our lives. Camps must create the best possible temporary communities and short-term experiences so that truth is communicated clearly, and campers are encouraged to respond. Campers need to learn and practice application skills while at camp and they need help transferring what they learn at camp to their lives at home. Camping leaders must encourage campers and guests to connect within their families and with local churches. Camps must encourage campers to accept personal responsibility for their ongoing spiritual development and apply what they have learned. When family and church support is not available, camps must be creative and diligent to find ways to help campers follow through and apply what they learned and committed to at camp.

Storms will always be a part of the human story. We must build our lives on the good foundation that comes from applying the truth of God's Word to our lives. And we must help our campers prepare for the storms that will eventually come their way. Camps provide a superb setting for concentrated Bible study and a wonderful place to practice applying God's truth to our lives. But effective camp ministries strive to help campers transfer the commitments of camp into strength and stability to face the challenges back home.

God uses camp experiences in the spiritual development of millions of people each year. But those short-term experiences are not an end unto themselves. They are designed to prepare campers to reengage their families, churches, and world with new perspectives and deeper commitments. Ultimately, we must all recognize the unique roles God has entrusted to us in the limited Christian camping arena and do the best we can. All the while remembering that God is at work fulfilling His master plan. Fortunately, God graciously allows us to participate in the work He is doing.

$A$fter this I looked, and there before me was a great multitude that no one could count, from every nation, tribe, people and language, standing before the throne and before the Lamb. They were wearing white robes and were holding palm branches in their hands. ¹⁰ And they cried out in a loud voice:

"Salvation belongs to our God,
who sits on the throne,
and to the Lamb."

¹¹All the angels were standing around the throne and around the elders and the four living creatures. They fell down on their faces before the throne and worshiped God, ¹² saying:

"Amen!
Praise and glory
and wisdom and thanks and honor
and power and strength
be to our God for ever and ever.
Amen!"

*Revelation 7:9-12*

### Chapter Twelve
# Victory Party
*Revelation 7:9-12*

The Apostle John was nearing the end of his life – and what a life it had been! His good job, working in the family fishing business, had been disrupted by an itinerate Rabbi many years earlier. For over three years, John had watched Jesus teach large crowds, confront hypocrites, heal the sick, feed thousands, still storms, love His enemies, and raise the dead.

Now, after a lifetime of loving and serving God, John had been banished to a cold dreary island where he was doomed to live out his remaining days in lonely isolation. He was the last remaining disciple of the Twelve who had followed Jesus; the only one left who had walked closely with Jesus during His years of earthly ministry.

In his remote seclusion, his mind drifted back to his travel and talks with Jesus. His days were filled with thoughts of bygone adventures and the hope for his heavenly reunion with Jesus. In the midst of these reflections, God's messenger came to John with a Revelation about the future. John's reflections on the past and his hope for eternity were interrupted with a grand and glorious glimpse of things to come.

This revelation included an astounding image of what awaits followers of Christ. John recorded, as best he could, the sights and sounds of a heavenly victory party.

*After this I looked and there before me was a great multitude that no one could count, from every nation, tribe, people and language, standing before the throne and in front of the Lamb. They were wearing white robes and were holding palm branches in their hands. And they cried out in a loud voice: "Salvation belongs to our God, who sits on the throne, and to the Lamb." All the angels were standing around the throne and around the elders and the four living creatures. They fell down on their faces before the throne and worshiped God, saying: "Amen! Praise and glory and wisdom and thanks and honor and power and strength be to our God for ever and ever. Amen!" (Revelation 7:9-12)*

Seven elements are worth noting in this spectacular vision of what awaits those who have a right relationship with God through His Son, Jesus. And it should come as no surprise there is a close connection to camp ministry and the grand and glorious party of Revelation 7.

## Immensity

This is a huge crowd. *A great multitude that no one could count* (v. 9). That's a big party! I'm sure that some denominational leaders will be amazed at who else is at the party (and possibly who is not), but this is a gigantic gathering. The imagery suggests that Jesus, the Good Shepherd, has been busy calling many sheep into His flock. Each year millions of campers attend Christian camps, hear and respond to the Gospel, learn to live the Christian life, and acquire ministry and leadership skills. The number is growing each year as Christian camping expands around the globe. Yes, there are many ministries that engage millions of people; education, music, health care, and local churches touch the most. But camp is where many people enter the party. Camp is the gateway for millions who will join the throng for this celestial celebration.

## Diversity

A diverse crowd assembles for the party, from every nation, tribe, people, and language (v. 9). Christian camping is expressed indigenously in most countries of the world. The economic, cultural, linguistic, and political realities in various parts of the world require Christian camping to emerge with different styles and methodologies. But everywhere, Christian camping finds ways to contextualize the five key pillars *(see Chapter 1)*. People need breaks from life's routines and pressures. They need new vantage points from which to assess their lives. They benefit from immersion in the beauty of God's creation. They enjoy deepening relationships with family and friends. And they refocus their lives around Christ. Despite these commonalities, Christian camping looks different in Kenya than it does Korea. The style of Christian camping in the Netherlands is different than what is found in Nicaragua. The language barrier alone divides many like-minded coworkers. The international sharing of information, resources, and training always takes place under the shadow of the curse of Babel. Even though the barriers are many, a wonderfully diverse crowd will someday assemble, and many will want to sing the songs they learned at camp.

## *Unity*

The crowd is unified around Jesus. The massive crowd *is standing before the throne and in front of the Lamb* (v. 9). No one is competing to get ahead of anyone else, but they are all straining to get closer to Jesus. He is the focal point of the party. Baptists, Presbyterians, Lutherans, Methodists, Quakers, Episcopalians, Catholics, and all the rest abandon their distinctives and shed every nonessential. All that matters is being close to Jesus. Camps are often the *Switzerland* of the Christian community; they provide *neutral* ground where theological differences do not alienate and divide, and denominational fine points are set aside. On the neutral ground of camp, people focus on the ultimate essential, Jesus Christ—who He is and what He has done.

---

*. . . the best singing at the biggest camp will never compare with the volume and voices of that heavenly choir.*

---

## Purity

Everyone encircling the throne is dressed in a white robe of purity. ***They were wearing white robes*** (v. 9). The great throng wears a common white uniform; they share the spotless perfection that none of them has earned but all of them have been given. All their stains are washed away, the dirt and grime of sin are gone. A sea of dazzling white robes, expressing the gift of purity. Cleansed by God's gracious gift, the white-robed and humbled crowd continually bursts forth with uproarious praise. Camp for many is the gateway to this new wardrobe. Camp is the place people are convicted of their self-centered hearts and their sinful rebellion against God. Camp is where they hear the good news of God's love demonstrated through the death of His Son, Jesus, and the power of God demonstrated in His resurrection from the dead. And camp is the place many put their faith in Jesus - the only pathway that leads them into a right relationship with God. He alone provides access to the white robes of purity.

## Praise

Palm branches were waved in praise to the Lord. *(They)* *were holding palm branches in their hands* (v. 9). Their joy and exuberance could not be contained; the celebration was overwhelming, and the party called for more and more delight. Palm branches that once honored Jesus as He rode into Jerusalem were again added to the majestic panoply. The singing was deafening; the roar resounded throughout the entire assembly. And the regal palm branches waved in concert with the singing, adding to the grandeur and splendor of that joyful event. Camps are places of joy. They are places of celebration and praise. But the best singing at the biggest camp will never compare with the volume and voices of that heavenly choir.

*That good news is not just that we hold a ticket to the festival, the good news is the reason we celebrate. Our unfettered celebration rejoices in who God is and what He has done—and that is cause for the biggest party of eternity.*

## Focus on God

Everyone proclaimed the same message. *And they cried out in a loud voice: "Salvation belongs to our God, who sits on the throne, and to the Lamb* (v. 10). The message of God's salvation was on everyone's lips. God is the source of our salvation. The focus is on God the Father who sits on the throne and His Son, Jesus Christ, the Lamb who was slain and rose again, triumphant over sin and death. That *good news* is not just that we hold a ticket to the festival. The *good news* is the reason we celebrate. Our unfettered celebration rejoices in who God is and what He has done---and that is cause for the biggest party of eternity.

The message that we are committed to is explained over and over at camp – the fifth pillar *(see Chapter 1)* of spiritual intents that align with the truth of God's Word. That good news is proclaimed in all-camp teaching sessions, small group Bible studies, campfires, cabin devotions, and one-on-one conversations. The message is central to the eternal celebration, central to our faith, and must remain central to our camps.

## Angels

The angels' participation is different from humans'. These supernatural beings engage the event from a slightly different entryway. *All the angels were standing around the throne and around the elders and the four living creatures. They fell down on their faces before the throne and worshiped God, saying: "Amen! Praise and glory and wisdom and thanks and honor and power and strength be to our God for ever and ever. Amen!"* (v. 11-12)

The angels do not come to the party through the portal of forgiveness. Unlike their demonic counterparts, holy angels never rebelled against God and never experienced the staggering loss of relationship with God or the astounding benefit of forgiveness that humans can enjoy. Jesus died for humans, not angels. The humans around the throne are focused on God's salvation and majesty, while the angels shine their spotlight only on the greatness of God's character: *majesty, glory and wisdom and thanks and honor and power and strength be to our God for ever and ever* (v.12).

---

 *The party celebrates both what God has done for us and the heart of who God is.*

---

Camp is about our response to the Gospel, but it is also about our response to God Himself. The two are intertwined but distinct, like the two sides of a coin. If we only thank God for what He has done but neglect praising Him for His essential character, we miss the wonder and magnificence of God. If we stand in awe of His attributes but neglect His work on our behalf, we miss the expression of His love for us and fail to grasp the simple yet singular pathway to connect with God. The party celebrates both what God has done for us and the heart of who God is.

## Conclusion

There are two simple yet profound connection points for camps today. *First,* at camp, celebrations foreshadow the joy and exuberance of that future party. Camp should be fun and filled with robust laughter. Camp should unashamedly provide mountain-top, emotional experiences that anticipate the victory party to come. And *second,* camp should provide many campers and guests with the priceless invitation to enter the party.

The joy and celebration of Christian camp mirrors, in a very minimal yet profound way, the euphoria that awaits. Some people criticize the mountain-top experiences of camp and complain about shallow, emotional commitments. That criticism signals a risk, but that concern should not deter us from striving to mimic, in a small way, the mountain-top party and the emotional outpouring that awaits.

Christian camps around the world provide the entryway into this celestial party. Many people are fitted for their pure white robes of forgiveness at camp. Retreats, camps, conferences, and adventure experiences are the places where the people of God, the love of God, the truth of God, and the grace of God intersect. And at that convergence – within the beauty of God's majestic creation – lives are changed forever and ever. Amen!

*Proceeds from BLUEPRINTS will support the*
*Christian camping movement around the world*

# Acknowledgements

I am deeply indebted to innumerable people who have helped shape my thoughts about Christian camping and who have given life to this little book. At the risk of overlooking some of the key players, I would like to mention a few who were vital in this process.

Don Anderson and Phil Hook were the first camp directors I served under at Pine Cove. Don was a great Bible teacher and a master at camp program design. Phil was a remarkable theologian, biblical scholar, and deep thinker. These two - along with scores of other Pine Cove staff, campers, and board members - helped me grapple with the biblical foundations of Christian camping.

Along the way, Don Goehner, Bob Kobielush, Bob Kraning, Jim Halls, Fred Miller, John Pearson, and so many more invested in my understanding of the United States' unique expression of the ministry we call Christian camping.

As my ministry migrated to the world stage, Ross Bay, Vic Brink, Robert Bruneau, Bruce Dunning, Lorimer Gray, Gerhard Hobelman, Muhia Karianjahi, Alexander Kharitonov, Christine Murison, Ken Pullen, Dave Tolman, and a host of others broadened and sharpened my awareness of various expressions within the global Christian camping movement.

Many people reviewed this work, providing proofreading, editing, and conceptual refinement. Leslie Strader, Paula Myers, Sara Holmes, Dan Smith, and Dan DeGroat helped significantly; any words that are spelled correctly and any sentence that applied standard rules of grammar are because of their assistance. Any errors are mine alone.

Marty Putman and Gwen Bowen helped process many of these thoughts while serving on staff at Christian Camping International – Worldwide. Lori Price worked tirelessly managing the details of this project, editing, designing, pushing back, and improving it in so many ways.

This project took so long that I used three offices, each supplied by nearby local churches, Bethel Bible Church in Tyler, Texas, Central United Methodist Church in Arlington, Virginia, and the Vietnamese American United Methodist Church, also in Arlington, Virginia.

The David Weekley Family Foundation provided the funding to produce this work in English, Russian, and Spanish. This generous support allows the proceeds to support the global expansion of Christian camping and to strengthen the movement.

The Refueling in Flight Ministries Board of Directors - Cay Bolin, Bedford Holmes, Brad Mercer, and Ken Sutterfield - offered guidance and encouragement during the years of writing and refinement. Their wisdom, friendship, and support has provided direction for this and many other Refueling in Flight projects.

My wife, Cay, deserves special thanks for putting up with me for 45 years while I have wrestled with these ideas. And for listening to me give talk after talk related to these subjects, always appearing genuinely interested. Her love and support makes this ministry possible.

# About the Author

Dan Bolin worked 25 years at Pine Cove Christian Camps near Tyler, Texas, serving first as cabin counselor, then program director, children's camp director, and for the final 14 years, as executive director. During that time, he spent 12 years on the Board of Directors of Christian Camp and Conference Association, two years as chair. For more than a decade, Dan worked as a senior consultant for the Goehner Group training and equipping numerous camping leaders in the United States and Canada. Dan invested the final 11 years of his career as the International Director of Christian Camping International. Within that role he trained and encouraged Christian camping leaders in more than 30 countries.

Currently Dan is the President of Refueling in Flight Ministries, a Christian nonprofit organization designed to support his speaking, writing, and event leadership.

He has authored eight books and spoken at numerous ministry conferences. He writes a weekly devotional blog - Refueling in Flight - and teaches Outdoor Ministries courses in academic and practitioner contexts.

Dan and his wife, Cay, live outside of Washington DC, near their daughter, son-in-law, and two delightful grandchildren.

For more information about Refueling in Flight Ministries or to subscribe to Dan's weekly devotional:   www.refuelinginflight.com

# Other Books by the Dan Bolin

*Invitation to Educational Ministry:*
*Foundations of Transformative Christian Education*
*(Chapter: Utilizing Retreats, Camps, & Outdoor Ministries)*
Hillman & Edwards, Kregal, 2018

*Fresh Bread*
Self-Published, 2016

*The Winning Run and Other Life Lessons from Baseball*
with Ed Diaz | NavPress – 1999

*A Hole in One and Other Life Lessons from Golf*
NavPress – 1999

*Avoiding the Blitz and Other Life Lessons from Football*
NavPress – 1998

*The One that Got Away and Other Life Lessons from Fishing*
NavPress – 1998

*How to Be Your Wife's Best Friend*
with John Trent | NavPress – 1994

*How to Be Your Little Man's Dad*
with Ken Sutterfield | NavPress – 1993

*How to Be Your Daughter's Daddy*
NavPress - 1993

# About Christian Camping International

The Mission of Christian Camping International (Worldwide) is to promote and support Christian camping throughout the world, as a means of serving the Church to fulfill the Great Commission of Jesus Christ.

The Vision of Christian Camping International is to be a highly effective and highly valued ministry tool throughout the world supporting a growing alliance of internally strong, sustainable, and growth-focused associations of Christian camps, conference centers, outdoor activity providers and their leaders.

Areas represented with CCI:

| | | |
|---|---|---|
| Albania | Korea | Romania |
| Australia | Latin America | Russia |
| Brazil | Nepal | Southern Africa |
| Canada | Netherlands | Spain |
| Eastern Africa | New Zealand | Ukraine |
| India | Pakistan | United Kingdom |
| Jamaica | Philippines | USA |
| Japan | Poland | |

For more information:

**www.cciworldwide.org**

# Finding *blueprints*

## Visit:
## <u>www.danbolin.com</u>

To purchase personal copies of **blueprints** both in the United States as well as around the world.

To purchase bulk discount copies of **blueprints** for your camp staff, organization, educational institution, board of directors or donors.

Purchase a "**blueprints** Bonus Box" to be donated to English speaking camping leaders and associations around the world.

FInd out about **blueprints** two specific language translation projects. Due to generous donors, **blueprints** has been translated into Russian and Spanish.

# Endnotes

### Chapter Two: God's Revelation

1   Urbanization, *Our World in Data* [website], https://ourworldindata. org/urbanization#long-run-history-of-urbanization (accessed 5 October 2021).

2   The fifth name, fear, may not fit the pattern precisely, but it does not detract from the primary thrust of the passage.

3   When Billy Graham Overcame Doubt at Forest Home, *Forest Home Christian Camps* [website], www.foresthome.org/a-small-moment-in-the-amazing-legacy-of-billy-grahams-ministry (accessed 5 October 2021).

### Chapter Five: Three Campers in Acts

4   I wish to acknowledge and thank Marcello Gualberto for introducing me to the three young people in the Book of Acts during a CCI-Brazil conference, circa 2008.

### Chapter Seven: The Complexity of Camp

5   Peter F Drucker, *Managing the Non-Profit Organization* (New York, New York: Harper Collins Publishing, 1990), xiv.

### Chapter Eight: Leadership Development

6   This quote has been attributed to both Vince Lombardi and General George Patton.

### Chapter Nine: A Ministry of Hospitality

7   I wish to acknowledge and thank Ken Pullen for introducing me to the principles of hospitality embedded in Genesis 18:1-8 during a CCI-Philippines conference, circa 2009.

### Chapter Ten: Program Versus Operations

8   Max DePree, *Leadership is an Art* (New York, New York: Dell Publishing, 1989), 11.

9   I'd prefer to use a different word than *serving*, or phrase than *physical serving*. Both speaking and physical activity are means of serving.

Printed in Great Britain
by Amazon

12718563R00123